First published in 2012

Copyright © John Bailey 2012

All rights reserved. No part of this publication may be reproduced, stored in a retrieval system or transmitted in any form, or by any means, electronic, photocopying, recording or otherwise without the prior permission in writing of the copyright holders.

www.countrysideprints.co.uk
e-mail info@countrysideprints.co.uk

ISBN 978-1-291-25736-6

THE HISTORY OF SKINHEAD REGGAE
1968 – 1972

JOHN BAILEY

'This book is dedicated to all the traditional skinheads of 69'

ACKNOWLEDGEMENTS

Well before we explore the golden age of reggae I would just like to say compiling the book has been a true labour of love. When I first made contact with Universal Music to enquire about the use of their images I was told that this was a work long overdue, a statement that came up time and time again in conversations, some by e-mail to Jamaica and some by the good old fashioned telephone. I would first of all like to acknowledge Emperor Rosko for his generous contribution of the foreword. When I asked him about his top ten he said "did I forget anyone, you bet, there was only room for ten so I keep my closing mention for the guy who eclipses everyone with more songs for my top ten than there is space for". The Emperor placed 'Let Your Yeah Be Yeah' by The Pioneers at number one and that leads very aptly to my thanks to Sydney, Jackie and George, who were a significant part of the golden age of reggae, for permission to use the photographs of the group within the book.

The chapter covering Toots and of course The Maytals has been enhanced with the quotes from Toots regarding the first reggae sound and the inspiration for him recording '54-46', a true skinhead classic and I thank Mike Cacia, Toots manager, for granting permission.

My appreciation goes out to Simon Lindsay and Samantha Hales for their time spent sorting permission to be granted for the images of all of the Trojan album covers and vinyl labels used in the book, the Trojan catalogue is now solely owned by Universal Music. Island Records were originally founded by Chris Blackwell and Graeme Goodall in Jamaica as far back as 1959 and are now part of Universal Music.

I would like to acknowledge the help from Nicola Kennedy for arranging the granting of permission for the use of all Island images in the book. Nicola also kindly arranged with Juliet Henzell, daughter of the late Perry Henzell, for her kind permission for the use of 'The Harder They Come' album cover and text.

My thanks go to Claire Tilley head of marketing at John Blake publishing for the use of the image from 'Want Some Aggro' by Cass Pennant and Micky Smith and for the permission to use an extract from the book, both remain © John Blake Publishing Ltd.

It has been a long but enjoyable haul contacting various people who were involved in the reggae scene back in the late 60s to get permission for images to be used and my thanks also go to Junior Lincoln in Jamaica for the inclusion of his Bamboo label.

I was delighted to include the words from Ian R Smith, member of The Inner Mind, described as 'the greatest white reggae band on earth' by Pama, telling of his experiences with Pama and other labels and how he formed his own Hot Lead label. Ian also provided a fascinating collection of posters from the golden age of reggae.

Chris Brown author of 'Booted and Suited' has also kindly recalled his memories of how we used to get hold of the music during those early years.

Whilst every possible effort has been made to ensure the copyright owners of any work have been traced, there may be some omission of credit to which I apologise, but the correct acknowledgement can be added to the book when appropriate.

They say that you should always leave the best 'till last, so therefore my final acknowledgments are to the artists and producers that brought us the golden age of reggae, the list is long and sadly as you may well know some have passed on. My gratitude goes out to The Pioneers, Max Romeo, Jimmy Cliff, Dave & Ansel Collins, Toots And The Maytals, Greyhound, Derrick Morgan, Dandy, Eric Donaldson, Lee 'Scratch' Perry, Bunny 'Striker' Lee, the list just goes on and on. I mention with a hint of sadness my posthumous appreciation to Desmond Dekker, Nicky Thomas, Judge Dread, Leslie Kong, and Clancy Eccles to name but a few for their immeasurable contribution to the golden age of reggae.

Best not to forget to give a mention for the 'Traditional Skinhead'.

There are many web sites that focus on skinheads and reggae and listed below are a few of them that I would like to acknowledge for their help:
www.skinheadbible.com
www.reggaenews.co.uk
© spirit of 69

All Trojan and subsidiary labels and album artwork licensed from and © Universal Music
All Island labels and album artwork licensed from and © Universal Music
CBS labels and album artwork licensed from and © Sony Music Entertainment
Bamboo and subsidiary labels © Junior Lincoln
Page 75 'A Dream' album cover licensed courtesy of www.urbanimage.tv
Page 145 Rhino sleeve images by kind permission of www.covers33.co.uk

Whilst every effort has been made to contact any potential copyright holders of the former Pama label, their subsidiaries and artwork the search has proved fruitless. I would however like to acknowledge the help in my relentless quest from Andrew Radix at Phoenix Music International (PMI) formerly Jet Star who now own the Pama labels, David Rodigan, Adrian Sherwood, The Apollo Club London, Michael De Koningh, author of 'Young Gifted & Black' and 'Tighten Up'. Also help from Ian R Smith who worked along with Pama during the golden years and The Pama Forum who have all endeavoured to unravel the mystery, all with the same result, that it is nigh on impossible to find any contact.

Upsetters and Pioneers left to right; Alva Lewis (Upsetters), Lee Perry (Upsett
Pioneers), Glen Adams and Aston Barrett (Upsetters) and Sydney Crooks (P

The Upsetters and Pioneers arrive in London during 1969
hoping for a white Christmas.
Image courtesy of The Pioneers.

Upsetters, hoping for

CONTENTS

Foreword	8
Introduction	10
Skinheads and Reggae	12
Symarip	16
Trojan Records	18
Pama	20
The Inner Mind	22
The Labels	24
A Musicians Tale	60
Tell It Like It Was	62
Desmond Dekker	64
Max Romeo	71
The Pioneers	77
Jimmy Cliff	86
Bob & Marcia	92
Nicky Thomas	97
Dave & Ansel Collins	102
Greyhound	107
Toots & The Maytals	114
Judge Dread	120
Chartbusters	122
Leslie Kong	152
Lee 'Scratch' Perry	154
Harry J	161
Dandy	165
Clancy Eccles	172
Eric Donaldson	175
Dennis Alcapone	178
U-Roy	182
Bob Marley & The Wailers	185
Johnny Nash	190
The Various Artists	194
The Albums	207
Tighten Up	208
Reggae Chartbusters	226
Club Reggae	238
Straighten Up	250
The Harder They Come	252
Conclusion	256

FOREWORD

Thanks for asking me to participate in this long overdue book, there is reggae and then reggae as it was, and before reggae blue-beat / ska!

I could just list the chart guys but there is so much more fun stuff out there so I will give you my top 10 list, these are songs I still play weekly! But to the student of music and the fan of reggae this book will be a treasure.

Thank you John for writing about music I call infectious! It grabs you and moves you without one being aware, one finds one tapping one's feet to the rhythm without thinking about it, I loved reggae the first listen.

I started off with blue-beat / ska in the 50s! I even put my first purchase on the 10 list!

Enjoy this and treasure it, a music bible for the worthy! The guys and gal's who partied at the Apollo club in London, just to mention one of the many will relive the good times with this book and many thanks for helping me enjoy the party scene so much.

And yes, to set the book straight I did play Wet Dream a few times before the Beeb banned it, (with a big grin on my face !)

Emperor Rosko

Emporer Rosko started his broadcasting career as a Pirate radio DJ although his first opportunity to broadcast came whilst in the US Navy where he presented a show on an aircraft carrier. He joined the pirate radio station, Radio Caroline, from a ship off the coast of England in 1966. There his pacey American style soon made Rosko one of the station's best loved DJs.

Rosko was then heard on Radio Luxembourg. Following his tenure on the pirate ships he became one of Radio One's first signings in 1967, initially recording shows in France for the Midday Spin programme. On his first Midday Spin show Rosko introduced himself like, 'I am the Emperor, the geeter with the heater, your leader, your groovy host from the West coast, here to clear up your skin and mess up your mind. It'll make you feel good all over'. He highlighted the new Motown, reggae, and rock music.

From 1970 he presented the Friday Roundtable where new records were reviewed by a panel, and had a Saturday lunchtime slot where you could always be assured to hear some reggae, at that time still an occasional event at the beeb. He stayed with Radio One until September 1976.

The Emperor has since been heard on the Classic Gold network and REM.FM, his programme being pre-recorded in California. He is currently running Rosko Radio, his own soul station on Live 365 at www.emperorrosko.co.uk

Emperor's top tunes

1. Let Your Yeah Be Yeah – The Pioneers
2. Red Red Wine – Tony Tribe
3. Double Barrel – Dave And Ansil Collins
4. Al Capone – Prince Buster / Emperor Rosko
5. Wet Dream – Max Romeo
6. Liquidator – Harry J Allstars
7. Wonderful World Beautiful People – Jimmy Cliff
8. Jamaican Ska – Ska Kings
9. Israelites – Desmond Dekker
10. Help Me Make It Through The Night – John Holt

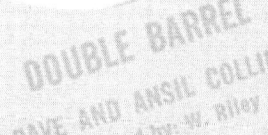

INTRODUCTION

The relationship between the original skinheads of the late 1960s and reggae music are often a source of debate, as to the uninitiated they seem curious partners. The raw unpretentious sounds of reggae, with the enduring overtones of rocksteady were in great contrast to the mainstream progressive rock and pop that was the mainstay of the BBC playlists at that time. The music was often first heard at the school disco as very little reggae received air play on the BBC. What is in no doubt by the summer of 69 skinheads and reggae were inseparable, a phase that was to last until 1972.

Reggae evolved in 1968, superseding rocksteady as Jamaica's dominant musical style, characterised by a guitar rhythm that accentuated the second and fourth beat in each bar, with the rhythm guitar either emphasising the third beat or holding the chord on the second beat until the fourth is played. The shift from rocksteady to reggae was pioneered by Bunny Lee with the organ shuffle sound featuring initially on Clancy Eccles 'Say What Your Saying' Lee 'Scratch' Perry's 'People Funny Boy' and the Pioneers 1967 track 'Long Shot Bus' Me Bet'. Early 1968 saw the release of the true reggae sound with 'Nanny Goat' by Larry Marshall and 'No More Heartaches' by The Beltones.

In 1969 a record produced by Bunny Lee would take the charts by storm and become an anthem for the skinheads. Despite the ban by the BBC Max Romeo's 'Wet Dream' reached number ten on the UK chart and was reputed to have sold over 250,000 copies. The two main players vying for success were Pama a label formed in 1967 by brothers Harry, Jeff and Carl Palmer with a base in North London and Trojan with a base in Neasden, North West London. Trojan was formed as a result of a tie in with Lee Gopthal's (B&C) and Island record owner Chris Blackwell, and would go on to release over 20 hit singles receiving plenty of air play. Their success with the British charts was thanks in the main to the skinheads embracing the music and adopting it as their own.

The book tells the story of the rise of reggae, and its followers, the skinheads from 1968 to its height, and subsequent demise as by the end of 1972 reggae had again evolved to what some say was, watered down and string laden. A far cry from the original raw sounds of the late 1960s which the remaining skinheads could no longer empathise. By the summer of 1972 the youth had moved on who had by now 'grown their hair a bit, not too long, and wore a baseball shirt, probably with a number seventeen on'.

All of the major artist of the time, some who have sadly passed on are reviewed with their singles and chart positions, their albums and of course the compilation budget LP's that were to become a mainstay, and a very important part of the skinheads collection. The leading producers of the day without whom none of this could have happened are also reviewed.

THE HISTORY OF SKINHEAD REGGAE 1968-1972   INTRODUCTION

The story ends with one of the most influential pieces of work ever to emanate from Jamaica, a masterpiece that would catapult reggae to the world stage, the feature film 'The Harder They Come', complete with its soundtrack, rightly said to be one of the most acclaimed compilation albums of reggae ever released.

By the summer of 69 skinheads and reggae were inseparable, a phase that was to last until 1972.

SKINHEADS AND REGGAE

Where did it all begin? Well we need to go back to the early 1960s, a time before the hippie movement when the British youths were divided into primarily two groups based on musical tastes. The mods had formed an allegiance to R&B and British rock bands like The Who and Small Faces; perhaps most significantly they had taken to Jamaican ska. The mods rode scooters and had a tendency toward dressing well. Their rival group with far more progressive musical taste, the rockers, rode motorcycles and wore leather jackets. When the psychedelic 1960s hit Britain the mods split into a wide variety of fashions and styles including hippies and the skinhead. This period is where the style of the skinhead was first defined. Skinhead fashion was intended to show a pride in the traditional English working-class look. The hard mod's who could not empathise with the hippie attitude and style got harder, and with a little influence from the Jamaican rude boys the traditional skinhead was born. The Jamaican ska the mods had endeared earlier in the decade, many now the elder brothers of the emerging skinheads, had slowed to the more romantic rocksteady rhythm, but by 1968 with poverty, violence and political unrest in Jamaica the music upped its tempo again and began to evolve into reggae.

Reggae can be distinguished from rocksteady by the slightly faster beat marked out by the drummer using the hi-hat, heavy organ lines, lower mixing of the bass, and electronically doubled rhythm guitar strokes. What was in no doubt by the summer of 69 skinheads and reggae were inseparable, a phase that was to last until 1972. Reggae during this period can be classified as skinhead reggae with the skinheads playing a major part in the promotion of the emerging sounds from Jamaica. For the first time Jamaican music was beginning to be noticed outside of the island. 1969 saw the new Jamaican music being bought in great quantities and enjoying an unrivalled success from international audiences, with reggae now charting in the UK.

As to who produced that first reggae sound is a matter of conjecture but certainly to the fore were The Maytals 'Do the Reggay' and Lester Stirling 'Bangarang' produced by Bunny Lee who has always claimed it as the first reggae record. In 1969 a record produced by Bunny Lee would to take the charts by storm despite the ban by the BBC. The record always referred to as "a record by Max Romeo" during a rundown of the charts was of course 'Wet Dream' reaching number ten and selling over 250,000 copies. The record was a huge hit for Pama who had released it on their Unity label UN-503. 1969 saw reggae emerge as a true force with one theory suggesting that the skinheads took to the raw unpretentious sound of reggae music as a reaction to the main stream music of the day, a statement that would reflect their fashion that had to some extent been copied from their black friends, including half mast trousers and almost shaven heads.

One of the most influential records was 'Skinhead Moonstomp' a single that was inevitably followed by the album of the same title. This was not however the first reggae record to bring together the skins and Jamaican music as in 1968 Dandy produced 'Skinheads A Message To You' a record released on Trojan's Downtown label DT-450 by Desmond Riley, but the embryo of the union between the music and the youth would have been Desmond Dekker's '007' and 'Israelites' both released on Pyramid.

The original skinheads were known as traditional skins having their own distinctive look of the era, they wore their hair cropped but not shaven, feathered was the order of the day for the skinhead girl. The look that set the skinhead apart was unique and consisted of a quality Ben Sherman shirt with button down collars, or a Fred Perry polo shirt, Levis 501 red tab jeans or Levi Sta-Prest trousers. I recall sitting in the bath with a brand new pair of Levi jeans on in order for them to shrink, to provide the classic skinhead tight look. The jeans were worn with the compulsory turn up of about an inch at the bottom so they sat at what was described as half mast, revealing the shine of your boots. Unlike the rude boys of Jamaica no matter how hard you were it was essential to have a coat for the winter in the UK, a Harrington jacket or Crombie overcoat if funds would stretch were the order of the day.

Levi Sta-Prest trousers were a relatively new brand that did exactly what it said on the label, they could be taken from the dryer, that is if you were fortunate to have had one back then, with no need to iron, and the creases did stay in. Levi Strauss & Co began production of these trousers as early as 1964. Mainly a khaki shade of green with two-tone becoming more popular as the era progressed. A Levi denim jacket was also an essential part of the skinheads wardrobe, with sleeves tucked up and the Levi badge taken from the inside and sewn above the left front chest pocket.

We must not forget the most essential part of the look, the half mast jeans were held up with braces about a half inch wide and crossed at the back. The appearance was complete with a pair of boots, originally hobnail, it didn't matter if they were DM's or not, but soon Dr. Martens were to become the preference. The eight and ten eyelet became popular and the Cherry Red look would often be courtesy of some vigorous polishing of a pair of brown DM's with ox blood or red polish. The Dr. Martens air filled soles were invented by a German doctor in the early 1960s with the original Dr. Martens boots coming into being during those early skinhead days. Brogues or loafers were also worn by the skinheads when the occasion suited.

Like most things today, the manufacturers were quick to take advantage of the skinhead uniform and what had been top quality clothing, including the Ben Sherman shirt and the Levi Sta-Prest trousers, began to be mass produced, flooding the market with far inferior garments, at odds to the original quality that had endured them to the skinheads. I am still the proud owner of my first Ben Sherman shirt and to this day the quality is unbelievable, looks and feels like new despite being over 40 years old, although it is not worn for a couple of reasons!

The skinheads had identified themselves to the rude boy culture of their new Jamaican friends and with their Dr. Marten boots, half mast Levis held up with bracers and cropped hair they looked formidable and intimidating to the masses.

Although they embraced the music and brought about its chart success they were also seen by some as influential in its downfall. In several interviews it has been well documented that Pama owner Harry Palmer has cited the influence of the skinhead on the record shop owners as damaging to the business. Many had refused to continue stocking the music Pama was producing for fear that their record shop would be overrun with the working class youth on a Saturday, a daunting proposition to other customers, causing a general loss of business.

The first skinheads also known as 'Traditional Skins' were influenced by Jamaican music and the Jamaican rude boys, following on from the mod movement. Unlike later generation that took the name the traditionalist skinheads of '69' were fashioned on those elements alone and did not regard attitudes toward racism and politics as central to their subculture, how could they be racist, many danced the night away with their new West Indian friends.

I recollect a story surrounding Max Romeo who had just finished a performance at a school in Guilford, including of course 'Wet Dream' to an audience of mainly white skinheads. On the way out a white man said something like, 'how you doing Mr Black', Max replied, 'alright Mr White', the man then spat at Max, the skinheads who were following Max turned and beat the white man up.

The sight of cropped heads and the sound of hefty boots entering the disco was enough to send many fleeing but the real aggro was reserved for the football terraces, a place where rival skinhead gangs, sometimes from the same clubs, ultimately aspired to be the hardest of them all. The aggro was well organised and each club had their own identity.

The book 'Want Some Aggro' tells of the time when skinhead gangs were staring out all over. Written by Cass Pennant and the late Micky Smith it tells the true story of West Ham's first Guv'nors from the late 60s to the early 70s. The following extract from season 69-70 is included with kind permission of John Blake Publishing Ltd.

"The Man U game came around and as planned about a hundred of us met up at Mile End at 10 o'clock. We got to the tube at Euston and waited around. About 12pm we knew the train was close because Old Bill started to appear and some sussed us out. We told them that we were Cockney Reds and were waiting for the main fans to come down as Upton Park was a bad place to go. They seemed to swallow this and, as there had been no aggro on the station, left us alone. We teamed up and decided to get them on the tube as it was too open at Euston and there were too many Old Bill around. Two trains came in and a massive mob of Man U got off, all chanting and letting people know that they were there- scarves, the lot. We let the first lot go and joined the second lot. Coming off the platform we all walked down to the tube and once on the train the Old Bill left. They had done their bit and it wasn't their problem anymore.

We waited for a couple of stations and then started. One of our lads nicked a Man U scarf and was trying to burn it with his lighter. The Man U fans didn't like that and about six of them fronted him. That was the signal. One bloke swung up on the overhead handles and kicked this Man U bloke in the face. He went down and the rest soon got a good slapping. As the train pulled into the station a load got off; the ones we had done got thrown off.

The train moved off and we went down to the next carriage. It was half packed with Man U fans and once we were all in, we steamed in. They were shouting and screaming. We just hit and kicked at them and trampled over them. At Tottenham Court Road station most of them pilled out and ran".

The aggro continued later on that day on the terraces inside Upton Park with several small scuffles breaking out, but nothing as violent and organised as was witnessed in the mid seventies, scenes that were replicated at many football grounds.

THE HISTORY OF SKINHEAD REGGAE 1968-1972   SYMARIP

By the dawn of 1971 many skinheads had grown their hair a bit and became known as suedeheads whilst some still maintained the style and others became boot-boys. Much of the disruption at football matches in the early 1970s was blamed on the skinhead culture, but in reality it was the clubs disciplined and well organised fans.

SYMARIP

Enter Symarip AKA The Pyramids, The Pyramids had launched themselves onto the UK music scene as Prince Buster's backing group during his earlier tours of the U.K.

The Pyramids recorded many singles including 'Feel Alright /Telstar' TR-7755 and 'To Sir With Love' TR-7770 both released on Trojan in 1970, they made a name for themselves as Symarip, one of the first reggae bands to target the skinheads. First to come was the single on Treasure Isle in 1969, 'Skinhead Moonstomp/Must Catch A Train' TI-7050, the former based on Derrick Morgan's 'Moon Hop'. The album was inevitable with a compilation released on Trojan in 1970.

The LP featured twelve boot-stomping tracks. 'Skinhead Moonstomp', 'Skinhead Girl' and 'Skinhead Jamboree' were all great stomping records with 'Chicken Merry' having a semblance to 'Long Shot'. A couple of instrumental's completed what was described at the time as the perfect party album. The original single sold well and an extensive tour of the UK followed with many venues thronged with 'stomping skinheads', 1970 saw the release on the Joe label JRS-9 by Joe The Boss titled 'Skinhead Revolt' with 'Skinhead Train' released on Explosion EX-2045 by The Charmers.

SKINHEAD MOONSTOMP   SYMARIP

TROJAN RECORDS TBL 102   Released 1970

Side 1
1. SKINHEAD MOONSTOMP 2. PHOENIX REGGAE 3. SKINHEAD GIRL
4. TRY ME BEST 5. SKINHEAD JAMBOREE 6. CHICKEN MERRY

Side 2:
1. THESE BOOTS ARE MADE FOR WALKING 2. MUST CATCH A TRAIN
3. SKIN FLINT 4. STAY WITH HIM 5. FUNG SHU 6. YOU'RE MINE

TROJAN RECORDS

The story of Trojan begins during 1967 when the label was set up as a platform for productions from Duke Reid. The name Trojan is believed to have its origin in Jamaica as the huge truck Duke Reid used to transport his sound system around was a seven ton Leyland 'Trojan' truck. The label soon folded but was resurrected to become reggae's biggest distributor in the UK by Lee Gopthall in 1968. Gopthall had been running a record store having had previous business connections with Chris Blackwell who had established Island records a decade earlier.

Reggae had hit the charts in the form of Desmond Dekker's 'Israelites' issued on the Pyramid label and Max Romeo's risqué 'Wet Dream' issued by Trojan's rival to be, Pama. Trojan's initial plan was to act as a feeder from Island Records releasing productions from Jamaica onto the UK market. The company enjoyed unparalleled success on the UK chart with hits from Lee 'Scratch' Perry's Upsetters, Desmond Dekker and Dave And Ansel Collins with their number one 'Double Barrel' in 1970.

The tracks were supplied from the likes of Duke Reid and Leslie Kong back in Jamaica with the singles transferred to budget priced LP's once potential sales had peaked. Trojan released the 'Tighten Up', 'Reggae Chartbusters' and 'Club Reggae' series that would become extremely popular with the growing fan base of skinheads who had embraced the music along with their new West Indian friends. Trojan had established over thirty subsidiary labels between 1968 and 1972 catering for the output from different producers. The highlights include Clandisc associated with Clancy Eccles, Duke Reid for Duke Reid productions, Downtown exclusively for Dandy, Harry J for Harry Johnson productions and Dynamic for releases from Byron Lee's Dynamic Jamaican studio to name but a few.

Why did it all go wrong as earlier in the decade Trojan was turning out an enormous amount of reggae and enjoyed several chart hits, but perhaps there lay the problem. Trojan began adding strings and horn arrangements to sweeten the sound aiming to appeal to the mainstream, a sound different to the one that had brought about the love affair with the skinhead, just listen to 'Long Shot Kick The Bucket', 'Return Of Django' or 'It Mek' all no nonsense raw sounds that the youth of the day could identify with.

Island pulled out of the partnership in 1971, a move that coincided with a declining interest in reggae.

Trojan Records had dominated the UK reggae market since their launch in 1968 to cater for the growing West Indian community and had released over 180 singles on various labels by the dawn of 1969. Traditionally Jamaican music, ska and rocksteady had found success in the singles market with LP's seen as a luxury item. Trojan revolutionised the album market launching a budget price series TTL in early 1969. Its inaugural release 'Tighten Up' was a compilation of the most popular recent releases, a format that would give wider access to the music, priced at just 14/6d.

It was a must have for the skinheads that had embraced the incessant dance music originating from Jamaica now being released in the UK. Those budget priced albums had a modest expectation from Trojan but would soon become a winning formula and the 'Tighten Up' series had arrived. With the success of 'Tighten Up' and the hits continuing on the chart an inevitable album was released titled 'Reggae Chartbusters' on the slightly pricier TBL series, a release that was to be the catalyst for another series, although running to just three volumes. Trojan's next series saw the release of 'Club Reggae' showcasing the hits that were popular in the clubs again with the same formula as Tighten Up with a compilation of recent singles where sales had peaked. The budget priced compilations proved a very popular choice with the record buying public. The reggae sales eventually began to suffer as the skinheads faded away and both Trojan and their rival Pama by the end of 1972 were releasing an extensive amounts of weak, watered down, string laden reggae which found no favour with the remaining skinheads or indeed the general record buying public, the love affair was well and truly over.

Trojan skinheads were influenced by the traditional late 1960s culture and were named after Trojan Records embracing Jamaican music and the rude-boy style. The logo 'Skinheads Against Racial Prejudice' was based on the Trojan Record logo with the helmet facing the opposite direction to the record company's logo.

Many stories have been told of the struggle of the artists in Jamaica and it was perhaps highlighted for the first time in 'The Harder They Come' when Ivan is offered very little for his song. The producer called the shots with both Trojan and Pama approached by the likes of Bunny Lee, Leslie Kong and Lee 'Scratch' Perry for their own label identifying their own work. At the height of the golden age of reggae Trojan and Pama alone accounted for over 40 labels, producing a staggering amount of music, this continued until production began to decline around 1971. It has been said that Trojan ensured the records most likely to succeed would be released on the their main Trojan imprint with this theory backed up with the success of Desmond Dekker, Jimmy Cliff, Bob & Marcia, The Pioneers and Greyhound, the main exception being Dave And Ansel Collins success on Trojan's Winston Riley's Techniques label.

PAMA RECORDS

Pama records were initially set up by the Palmer brothers, Harry, Jeff and Carl releasing singles from the sixties into the seventies. The original output was soul based recordings but the label became a major outpouring for reggae with the transition beginning in 1967. Pama began issuing rosksteady singles from Jamaican producers such as Clancy Eccles, Bunny Lee, Laurel Aitken and Lee 'Scratch' Perry.

The label unlike its competitor Trojan only enjoyed one top ten hit, but what a hit it was, produced by Bunny Lee and released on the Unity label. 'Wet Dream' by Max Rome took the charts by storm in 1969 with its risqué lyrics never receiving any airplay (apart from the outings courtesy of Emperor Rosko) but still sold over 250,000 copies and remained on the UK charts for a respectful twenty five weeks. Another hit for Pama was Derrick Morgan's 'Moon Hop', released on the Crab label with the record soon establishing itself as a favourite with the emerging skinheads, reaching number 49 in the UK chart. That same week saw Desmond Dekker And The Aces 'Pickney Gal', Boris Gardiner's 'Elizabethan Reggae', Jimmy Cliff's 'Wonderful World Beautiful People' and Harry J All-Stars 'Liquidator' all featuring.

It was no secret that a great rivalry existed between Pama and Trojan, a contention that had been fuelled by Bunny Lee who had licensed Derek Morgan's 'Seven Letters' to both companies. Like Trojan, Pama had several subsidiary labels, including Unity and Crab associated with Bunny Lee and the Punch label for the output from Lee 'Scratch' Perry. When Trojan introduced the very successful 'Tighten Up' series Pama responded with their own version aptly titled 'Straighten Up'.

The breakthrough came for Pama when Harry Palmer established a link with the Jamaica producer, one Bunny Lee, who was able to supply almost unlimited material that had already achieved success on his Jamaican Unity label. The second release on the Unity label in the UK was 'Last Flight To Reggae City' by Stranger Cole then came 'Bangarang' which had proved to be a massive hit in Jamaica often cited as the first reggae record.

The fourth issue was the up-tempo melodic, often described as ribald by the media, 'Wet Dream' UN-503. Additional labels were then launched with the emergence of Crab and Gas.

Bullet   Camel   Crab   Escort   Gas
Boss Sounds On Pama
Nu Beat   Ocean   Pama   Pama Supreme   Punch   Success   Supreme   Unity

Further labels followed including Escort probably best known for the original issue of Bob & Marcia's 'Young Gifted And Black' a version with no strings attached. Bob Andy was said to be surprised when it was issued by Pama along with some concern from Trojan, as a result it was hastily replaced on the same label and number with a somewhat uninspiring version from Denzil And Jennifer. What followed has been well documented with the release being put out by Trojan complete with the string arrangement by Johnny Arthey, the record becoming an all time classic hit. The record did however emphasize the difference in the reggae to come out over the next couple of years as it had highlighted that Trojan were prepared to sweeten tracks with strings added to ensure success in the pop market.

The most distinctive label to emerge from the Pama stable was without doubt the Punch label. The design portrayed a fist smashing into the top 20 chart with the label initially concentrating on the sounds that were gripping the skinheads. One was the follow up to the Upsetters 'Return Of Django', 'Clint Eastwood' a record that it was claimed if distribution had not hampered its progress would have been another chart success for Pama. Another record that was issued on both Pama's Punch label and Trojan was Dave Barker's 'Shocks of Mighty' although Barker was said to have been unaware of the Pama issue. Increasingly with the same artist appearing on both Pama and Trojan several singles were released simultaneously although it would be covered up by a change of title and artist on the credits. Other labels in competition with the big two at the time were Junior Lincoln's Bamboo and Melodisc.

By the end of 1971 the companies production from Jamaica was begin to dry up with Trojan now fully established as the main producer with several chart successes to their name. The sound originating from Pama and its subsidiaries still held true to the unpretentious sounds that had earlier catapulted reggae to the fore back in 1968, unlike its rival Trojan. However by 1972 only Bullet, Camel, Pama Supreme, Punch and the main Pama label remained from the heyday of a dozen or so subsidiaries, all turning out vast amounts of reggae singles, and several albums. The company would survive beyond 1972 but by 1974 had gone out of business. The 'Straighten Up' series that Pama had launched to rival Trojan's innovative compilation series of budget albums 'Tighten Up' ran to just three volumes issued through to the end of 1972 with other compilations titled 'This Is Reggae' and 'Hot Numbers'. To the skinhead and the collector of reggae the label had come to personify a certain sound, ask any reggae connoisseur from 68-72 about a label and they would identify the sound and the producer, for it was the producer who was king at that time.

THE INNER MIND

During the late 60s there were a handful Jamaican musicians living in London who would support stop-over recording stars from Jamaica on tour, including the likes of Prince Buster. By 1969 with reggae now charting other artists arrived in Britain with Desmond Dekker leading the way, although The Aces refused to travel with him. Within a few months the bustling capital became home to Derrick Morgan, Jimmy Cliff, Owen Grey and of course Laurel Aitken.

Most of the artists were unknown in Britain, apart that was from their recording talents and many a promoters tale has been told of the same artist topping the bill at different far apart venues on the same night.

The backing for many of the artists new UK releases were from British based musicians and one group from Yorkshire 'The Inner Mind' were destined to become one of Pama's backing bands, earning the title as 'the greatest white reggae band on earth'. The group had formed in 69 and comprised Ian R Smith, Organ and Piano, Jimmy Walsh on drums, Dave Tattersall, bass and Finley Topham guitar. Ian generously reveals his personal recollections during the golden age of reggae later in the book, 'a musician's tale'.

The Inner Mind backed many of Pama's established reggae acts such as Laurel Aitken, Owen Gray, Winston Groovy and Alton Ellis.

Their first release was an instrumental on the Shades label SHA11 'Dreams Of Yesterday' a track that did receive extensive air play including outings on Radio One, but in those days distribution and promotion was atrocious, preventing records being available to larger audiences, holding the record back unlike Trojan who had enjoyed their extensive network of connections.

Fledgling record companies began to emerge and one was Ian R. Smith's Hot Lead Records based in Yorkshire. The Inner Mind had releases on Pama's New Beat label with one of their biggest in 1970 'Pum Pum Girl' NB069 although erroneously credited to Laurel Aitken on the label, and singles on Bullet, BU465 in 1971 Arawack Version and Devil Woman BU490 the same year.

Pama also released an unauthorised record on the Pama Supreme label PS352 in 1972 titled 'Breakdown Rock' which just happened to be 'Dreams Of Yesterday' crediting the artist as The Harlesden Monks. Without doubt Ian Smith's biggest success came in 1973 after the skinhead era had subsided with the release on Hot Lead of 'Doggie Bite Postman' under the guise of 'Smithy' a record that it was said to have sold faster than it could be pressed, a brilliant risqué version of 'Maga Dog' HL12 the B side featuring an instrumental version 'Teeth Marks' very reminiscent of skinhead reggae at its best.

The Inner Mind were described as the 'greatest white reggae band on earth'.

The history of the labels up next makes a fascinating read and their influence during the golden age should never be understated.

THE HISTORY OF SKINHEAD REGGAE 1968-1972   THE LABELS

THE LABELS

TROJAN

AMALGAMATED
(PREFIX) AMG

The label was set up in 1968 by B&C to issue production from Joe Gibbs.

The most notable recordings were from The Pioneers including such classic offerings as 'Long Shot', 'Jackpot' and 'Mama Look Deh'. The label also issued 'Wreck A Buddy' by The Soul Sisters and 'Them A Laugh And A Ki Ki' by The Soulmates both featuring on Tighten Up Volume 2 TBL 132 in 1970, a re-release of TTL 7 originally released during 1969. The first single on the Amalgamated label was 'Please Stop Your Lying' by Errol Dunkley AMG-800. Amalgamated continued to produce over seventy good quality recording right up until early 1971 with Joe Gibbs production switched to the Pressure Beat label created in 1970.

ATTACK
(PREFIX) ATT

Graeme Goodall launched the Attack label in 1969.

The label initially concentrated on British reggae with The Pyramids in their various guises having the lion's share of the production. The label ceased production in 1970 with just a mere twenty three records ever being released before the label folded. It was however to be revived by Trojan in 1972 seeing some good quality releases including 'Scorpion' and 'Do It Again' by Lloyd & Carey, and 'Starting All Over Again' by Hopeton Lewis. The label was to continue record production for Trojan well into the decade.

BIG
(PREFIX) BG

Rupie Edwards was the main producer for the Big label with perhaps its most notable offering from The Gaylads, 'Can't Hide The feeling' a track featured on Club Reggae Volume 2 and an offering from Max Romeo 'Are You Sure'. The label ceased production at the end of 1972 perhaps not one of Trojan most significant contributors.

THE HISTORY OF SKINHEAD REGGAE 1968-1972   THE LABELS

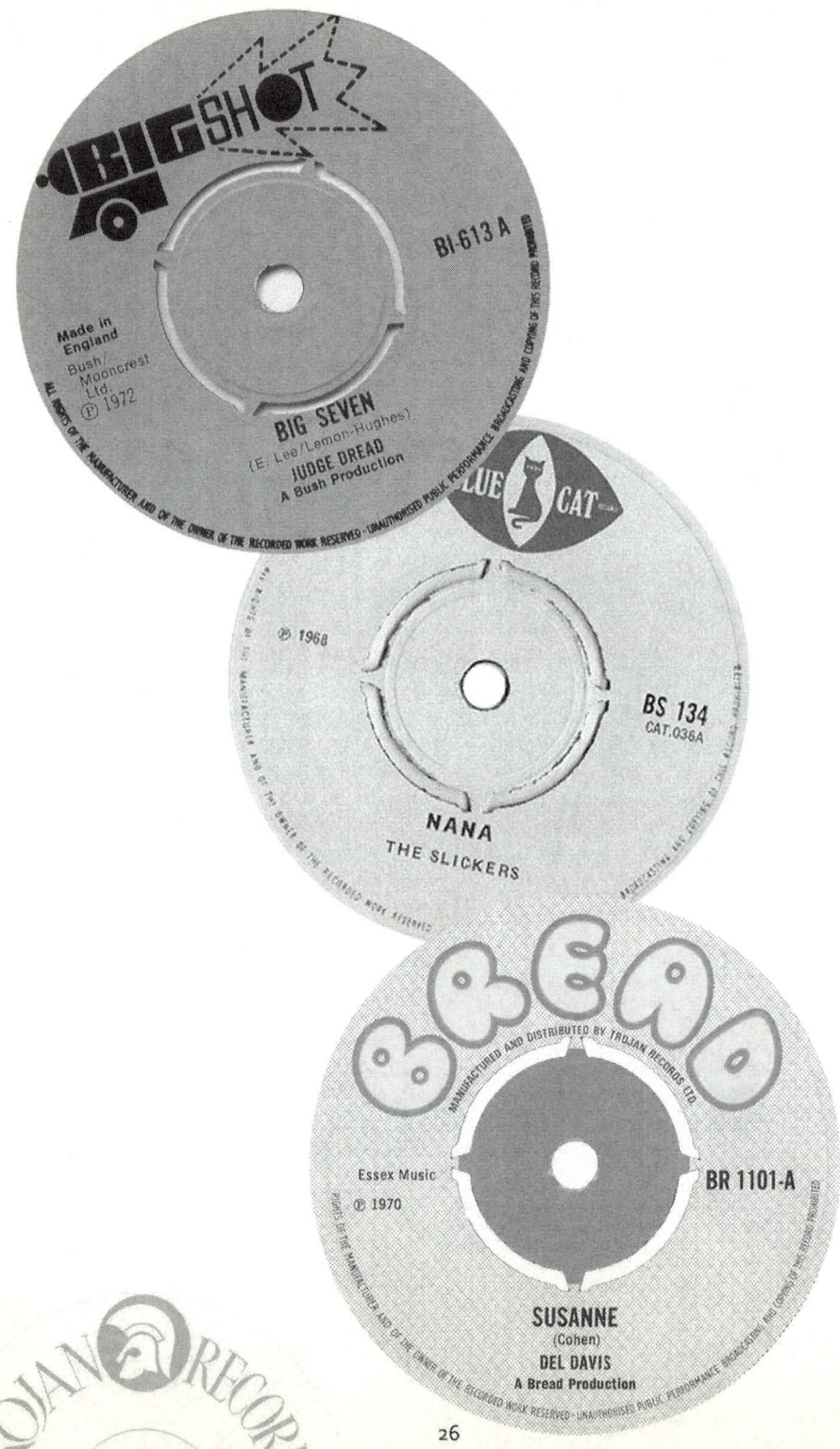

BIG SHOT
(PREFIX) BI

The first release on Big Shot was 'Reggae Girl' BI-501 in late 1968, at the dawning of the golden age of reggae. The label would go on to release over one hundred and twenty singles. Two of the labels early offering would feature on the highly acclaimed Tighten Up Series, 'Sufferer' by The Kingstonians and 'John Jones' by Rudy Mills on volume 2 with a later release by Niney 'Blood & Fire' featuring on Volume 4. 1972 would see the release of the labels British chart success in the shape of 'Big Six' and 'Big Seven' by Judge Dread.

BLUE CAT
(PREFIX) BS

Blue Cat was a label launched in 1968 only lasting until 1969 but issuing over fifty singles in the first year.

'Nana' by the Slickers and a couple of tracks by The Maytones 'Billy Goat' and 'Loving Reggae' are the singles that stand above the other releases. During the final few releases the label design changed to a more traditional white and orange Trojan style design.

BREAD
(PREFIX) BR

Trojan established Bread in 1970 as a label for Jackie Edwards productions. The labels output was leant toward the commercial sound with the most notable singles being 'Johnny Gunman', a track featuring on Club Reggae Volume 3, 'Your Eyes Are Dreaming' by Danny Ray and Jackie Edwards and BR-1108 'I Do Love You' C/W 'Who Told You So?' by Jackie Edwards. The label would issue just twenty singles ceasing production in 1973.

THE HISTORY OF SKINHEAD REGGAE 1968-1972   THE LABELS

CLANDISC
(PREFIX) CLA

The name should be easily identified with the legendary Clancy Eccles. The label was launched by Trojan in 1969 and has to be one of the most notable for quality recordings. The label was to offer a mix of productions and releases by Clancy Eccles including 'Herbsman Shuffle' by King Stitt and 'Unite Tonight' by Clancy Eccles, superb offerings that would go on to feature on the Tighten Up series. 'Holly Holy' by The Fabulous Flames and 'Sweet Jamaica' sung admirably by Clancy, both excellent tracks would feature on the Club Reggae Volume 1 and Volume 2 respectfully. Other notable offerings were 'Open Up' by Clancy and 'Rod Of Correction' another offering from Clancy, the later another track to feature on the Tighten Up series, this time Volume 5 in 1972.

DOWNTOWN
(PREFIX) DT

Downtown was set up in 1968 exclusively for Richard Thompson, better known as Dandy, RLT or Boy Friday to name but a few. The label not only issued productions by Dandy but also his excellent offerings including, 'Move Your Mule' and 'Reggae In Your Jeggae'. One of the most notable singles was DT-419 released in 1969, 'Red Red Wine' by Tony Tribe, with some copies crediting the recording to Tony Tripe, imprinted on the label instead of Tony Tribe. 'Skinhead A Message To You' calling for calm was issued on DT-450 by Desmond Riley with Dandy and Audrey forming a duet for 'Morning Side Of The Mountain'. Dandy moved onto record on the Horse label in the guise of Dandy Livingstone, a move that would see him enjoy success in the British charts, almost at the end of the golden era in the autumn of 1972.

THE HISTORY OF SKINHEAD REGGAE 1968-1972   THE LABELS

DUKE
(PREFIX) DU

The Duke label was formed in 1968 to issue productions from Duke Reid.

The Duke label ranks amongst the best for a variety of releases with undoubtedly the biggest success in terms of sales going to Boris Gardner's 'Elizabethan Reggae' DU-39 reaching number 14 in the British charts in March 1970. Quality recording are not the monopoly of the charts and the label boasted many fine offerings ranging in styles from Clancy Eccles 'Auntie Lulu' C/W 'Bag A Boo', 'Home Without You' by The Beltones, 'The Law' by Andy Capp, a track that featured on Club Reggae, 'Geronimo' by The Pyramids and 'To The Fields' by Herman, another track that was to feature on the early Club Reggae albums. 'Bald Headed Teacher' from Max Romeo and 'Save The Last Dance For Me' by The Heptones shows just how varied the offering was. The label ceased production in 1973.

DUKE REID
(PREFIX) DR

The label became an outlet for Ewart Beckford, better known as reggae's greatest deejay U.Roy or sometimes Hugh Roy. The originator as he was known had an excellent stream of offering on Duke Reid despite the label only releasing twenty four singles. The limited number of releases contributed to the labels production of first class reggae issued from 70 to 72. U.Roy was responsible for a third of the output with such classic tracks as 'Wake The Town', 'Wear You To The Ball' and 'Version Galore'. Another notable offering came from Hopeton Lewis with 'Boom Shacka Lacka' a track that also featured on Club Reggae.

THE HISTORY OF SKINHEAD REGGAE 1968-1972   THE LABELS

DYNAMINC
(PREFIX) DYN

Dynamic was launched as the UK outlet for producer Byron Lee who owned the Dynamic Studios back in Jamaica. Other producers used the label including Lee Perry and Bunny Lee who were also using Lee's studio back in Jamaica. The most notable and by far the best selling single was 'Cherry Oh Baby' the 1971 festival winner from Eric Donaldson released on DYN-420, a record produced by Bunny Lee. The outstanding offerings included several other tracks from Eric including, 'Blue Boot', 'Miserable Woman' and 'Love Of The Common People', the latter featured as the backing track for another inspired offering from Dennis Alcapone, 'Alcapone's Guns Don't Bark'. 'Johnny Too Bad' by the Slickers was another gem, a track that would feature on the forthcoming soundtrack of the feature film 'The Harder They Come'.

EXPLOSION
(PREFIX) EX

The name Explosion conjures up a real foot stomping vision, but the leaning was toward the commercial sounds, with very few tracks standing head and shoulders above the seventy or so singles released from 69 to 72. 'Man From Carolina' by The GG Allstars who were in fact The Slickers, 'Skinhead Train' by The Charmers and an offering from Neville 'I Love Jamaica', a reggae backing with a calypso slant on the vocals also produced by Neville, and Slim Smith's, 'The Time has Come' are though worth a spin.

GG
(PREFIX) GG

GG was producer Alvin Ranglin's main outlet on Trojan.

The label featured Verne & Son's 'Little Boy Blue' who's rhythm track would reappear later on the ribald offering from Judge Dread, 'Big Six'. A large contribution came from The Maytones with some of their best in the form of 'As Long As You Love Me' and 'Black & White'. Good reggae sounds came from Charlie Ace with 'Ontarius Version', 'Lonely Nights' Eric Donaldson and Max Romeo pops up showing his vocal talents with a complete change of course from 'Wet Dream' with 'Is It Really Over'.

THE HISTORY OF SKINHEAD REGGAE 1968-1972   THE LABELS

GRAPE
(PREFIX) GR

The label was set up in 1969 to release producer Joe Sinclair's work. Just a few notable tracks stand out with some of the earlier offering appealing to the skinheads with 'Skinhead A Bash Them' by Claudette & The Corporation and 'Guns Of Navarone', Freddie Notes & The Rudies. Another fine fast moving excellent dance crasher was 'Come Down' from Lloyd & Carey.

GREEN DOOR
(PREFIX) GD

The label kicked off in 1971, a relatively late starter but delivered some classic tracks that were released during 71 to 72. The backbone of the output erred toward pure Jamaican with the first release reflecting the emerging sound of roots from The Charmers, 'Rasta Never Fails'. The labels list of artists reads like a who's who of reggae and included Ken Boothe and The Heptones with 'Lively Up Yourself' and 'Guava Jelly' both offerings from Bob Marley & The Wailers. The quality did not stop there with 'Hypocrite' from The Heptones, 'A Sugar' by Roy Shirley, and 'President Mash Up The Resident' from Shorty.

HARRY J
(PREFIX) HJ

The iconic Harry J label was established to release the UK production from Harry Johnson, with the labels two most famous chart hits being, HJ-6605 'Young Gifted And Black' by Bob & Marcia and HJ-675 'Liquidator' by Harry J Allstars, the later appeared on Trojan 600 series TR-675 but with a Harry J label. Late 1972 saw the release of the upbeat 'Come Back And Stay' by The Fabulous Five and 'Down Side Up' again by Harry J Allstars, the tracks featuring on Club Reggae Volume 3 and Tighten Up Volume 6 respectively.

THE HISTORY OF SKINHEAD REGGAE 1968-1972   THE LABELS

HIGH NOTE
(PREFIX) HS

High Note was mainly launched for the release of material from producer Sonia Pottinger. Notable releases are 'ABC Rocksteady' by the Gaylads HS-001, 'Stay A Little Bit Longer' from Delano Stewart, a track featured on Tighten Up Volume 3 and 'Joy To The World' by Julie Ann (actually Judy Mowatt) & the Chosen Few. The track went on to gain an outing on Tighten Up Volume 5 (where it is credited to Julien & The Chosen Few). 'Dance With Me' from Delano Stewart and The Hippy Boys and 'Reggae Pressure' are also worthy of a mention.

HORSE
(PREFIX) HOSS

The label was seen by Trojan as a pop label very much aimed at the mainstream rather than the skinheads. Its most notable release has to be 'Suzanne Beware Of The Devil' HOSS-16 from one Dandy Livingstone towards the end of 1972. Very little of the labels offering would make it onto an album of purist reggae; however that was the labels intention from the outset. A couple of tracks worth a mention would be John Holt 'The Further You Look' HOSS-22 and a sublime reggae version of 'Tchaikovsky Piano Concerto No 1' by The Neasden Connection HOSS-17 produced by Robert Thompson AKA Dandy.

J-DAN
(PREFIX) JDN

The label lasted only a year set up by Trojan as a sister label to Dandy's Downtown. Only seventeen singles were released but none stand out as classic tracks. Most of the production came from the Music Doctors and Boy Friday, not surprising given they are pseudonyms for Dandy.

THE HISTORY OF SKINHEAD REGGAE 1968-1972   THE LABELS

JACKPOT
(PREFIX) JP

Jackpot ran similar to Pama's Unity label being the UK version of Bunny Lee's Jamaican Jackpot label. That said the label had few outstanding releases, however one exception was Delroy Wilson's 'Better Must Come' JP-763, a song used by the Jamaican PNP in 1972 during their successful election campaign. The track proved worthy of an outing on Trojan's Tighten Up Volume 5. Other tracks worthy of a mention include the 1972 release 'Guilty' by Ken Parker, a cover of the single by Tiger originally released on Pama's Camel label a year earlier and 'Girl Of My Dreams' from Dave Barker.

JOE
(PREFIX) JRS

The Joe label was aimed squarely at the rapidly emerging skinheads although the output only ran to seventeen singles with the release of tracks such as 'Trial Of Pama Dice', 'Skinhead Revolt' and 'The Informer'. All the releases in the series were produced by Joe Mansano who ran a record shack in Brixton.

MOODISC
(PREFIX) MU

Harry Mudie productions were released on Moodisc from 1970 to 1971 having previously issued work through Trojan's rival Pama. Cornel Campbell & The Eternals 'Let's Stay together' and an early release from I Roy 'Musical Pleasure' are two that are noticeable.

THE HISTORY OF SKINHEAD REGGAE 1968-1972   THE LABELS

PRESSURE BEAT
(PREFIX) PR

Pressure Beat had a limited amount of releases continuing from where Joe Gibbs Amalgamated label left off. Perhaps the most notable being 'Them A Fe Get A Beatin' Peter Tosh PB-5509 in 1972.

RANDY'S
(PREFIX) RAN

The label was launched in 1970 to issue production from the late Vincent Chin's Jamaican Randy's and Impact labels. Randy's feature high on the list of Trojan's subsidiary labels with a reputation for some excellent offerings. Jimmy London & The Impact Allstars featured with 'Bridge Over Troubled Water' released in 1971 on RAN-517 making it onto Trojan's Tighten Up Volume 5. An instrumental version had been released the previous year credited to Randy's Allstars on RAN-507. The equally impressive follow up to 'Bridge' was 'A Little Love' RAN-520 a track that really showcased the vocal talents of Jimmy. The Impact Allstars featured once again with Rocking Horse on 'Hard Time' RAN-522 a track featured on the eagerly awaited 1972 release, Club Reggae Volume 3.

SMASH
(PREFIX) SMA

Another label launched to act as an outlet for a Jamaican label in the UK, this occasion it was supposed to be Bunny Lee's Smash label. Things did not seem to go to plan although the label did have a couple of exceptionally good releases including 'Hard Life' with a heavily accentuated rhythm from Marlene Webber on SMA-2322 with the track featured on Tighten Up Volume 4 and 'Wake The Nation' from Hugh Roy on SMA-2313.

THE HISTORY OF SKINHEAD REGGAE 1968-1972   THE LABELS

SONG BIRD
(PREFIX) SB

The label launched in 1969 was initially given over in the main to Lloyd Charmers productions and Trojan's own Joe Sinclair. The early releases included 'Riding For A Fall' Derrick Harriott SB-1013 and 'Singer Man' SB-1019 by the Kingstonians a track to feature on Tighten Up Volume 3. Derrick Harriott featured again with 'Groovy Situation' SB-1042, later released on Trojan TR-7887 and featured on the first Volume of Club Reggae. 'Good Ambition' by The Ethiopians, 'Riddle I This', Scotty & Derrick, 'Know For I' Bongo Herman & Bunny and 'Lot Wife' SB-1062 by The Ethiopians are all excellent tracks that would find their way onto any best of album.

SPINNING WHEEL
(PREFIX) SW

Launched in 1970 the label released less than a dozen singles and folded after just a year.

SUMMIT
(PREFIX) SUM

Summit was launched to provide Trojan with an outlet for work from the up and coming Leslie Kong's Beverley's Records in Jamaica. Following Leslie Kong's sudden death in August 1971 Trojan continued releasing his work posthumously but when these ran out so did the labels direction. The excellent work from Leslie Kong is clear to see on the labels output with the classic tracks including The Melodians 'Rivers Of Babylon' SUM-8508 and The Pioneers 'Starvation' SUM-8511. The Maytals 'Monkey Girl' SUM-8513 and their 'One Eye Enos' SUM-8520 were also classic reggae of the highest standard as was a cover of Dawn's 'Knock Three Times' by Brent Dowe, and 'It's You' and 'Walk With Love' again from The Maytals.

THE HISTORY OF SKINHEAD REGGAE 1968-1972   THE LABELS

TECHNIQUES
(PREFIX) TE

Winston Riley productions were showcased on the Techniques label launched in 1970. The highlight of not only the label but for Trojan was the release of TE-901 'Double Barrel' by Dave & Ansel Collins, with the follow up TE-914, 'Monkey Spanner' both providing massive hits in the UK. The remainder of the output from the label was eclipsed by those two gems from Dave Barker & Ansel Collins.

TREASURE ISLE
(PREFIX) TI

Treasure Isle was an Island label from 1967 to 1968. Re launched by Graeme Goodall's Doctor Bird group in 1969. Treasure Isle began with the early releases featuring the skinhead anthem 'Skinhead Moonstomp' on TI-7050 and 'Pop A Top' by Andy Capp TI-7052. Phyllis Dillon's TI-7058 ' One Life To Live, One Love To Give' and 'Everybody Bawlin' TI-7064 by U.Roy & The Melodians are the most notable offerings of classic reggae released in 1971 when the label came under the direct control of Trojan, who were then dealing with Duke Reid productions.

TROJAN
(PREFIX) TR 600 SERIES & TR 700 SERIES

The second in Trojan's series, the first output from 1967-1968 putting out Duke Reid Productions. The second (600 series) on an orange label ran from 1968 through to the end of 1969 releasing a century of singles. The series began with some fine work by Dandy prior to the launch of his Downtown label. The first release was 'Donkey Returns' by The Brother Dan Allstars TR-601 released in July 1968. For the remainder of 1968 the label released some memorable tracks including, 'Spanish Harlem' Val Bennett TR-611, 'Tighten Up' by The Untouchables TR-613, 'Place In The Sun' by David Isaacs TR-616 and 'Stir It Up' by Bob Marley & The Wailers TR-617, many of which featured on Trojan's first budget priced compilation, Tighten Up. Between the end of 1968 and December 1969 a tremendous amount of quality material was released.

THE HISTORY OF SKINHEAD REGGAE 1968-1972   THE LABELS

46

The highlights including amongst many The Pioneers 'Long Shot Kick The Bucket' TR-672 which appeared on both the orange and orange and white labels, and their 'Poor Rameses' TR-698 on the orange and white label.

The (700) series continued where the predecessor (600) had left off with more top quality recordings including several productions from Leslie Kong and Duke Reid, but the beginnings of the sweetening process had begun. Trojan who were by now regularly gaining chart success with artist like Desmond Dekker, Jimmy Cliff and The Pioneers saw the label undertake another change, this time to its familiar 'brown shield' design. To sweeten the music Trojan had acquired the services of Johnny Arthey to add strings and orchestras, with perhaps the effect easily recognised on the UK versions of 'Young Gifted And Black' by Bob And Marcia and 'Love Of The Common People' by Nicky Thomas TR-7750, when compared with the original Jamaican recordings.

TROJAN
(PREFIX) TR 700 SERIES (BROWN SHIELD)

By late 1971 most of the singles released were on the brown shield design with occasional orange and white label designs being released, now with the popular single sleeve depicting the Trojan warrior. Most notable releases during this time, a time when reggae had evolved a long way from the early rocksteady influenced beat with regular chart success becoming short lived were to be Bob & Marcia with 'Pied Piper' issued on TR-7818, The Pioneers 'Let Your Yeah Be Yeah' issued on TR-7825 and Greyhound 'I Am What I Am' TR-7853.

TROJAN MAXI
(PREFIX) TR

Singles with two tracks on the B side were occasionally issued under the label of Trojan Maxi. The TR number followed on in the 700 series until 1972 when Trojan Maxi Singles were launched carrying a TR 900 prefix, mainly releasing compilation of previous hit singles. 'Moon River' by Greyhound TR-7848 made number 12 in the UK chart in February 1972 with the B side featuring 'I've Been Trying' coupled with 'The Pressure Is Coming On'.

THE HISTORY OF SKINHEAD REGGAE 1968-1972   THE LABELS

UPSETTER
(PREFIX) US

One of the most identifiable of Trojan's subsidiary labels set up for the output from Lee 'Scratch' Perry in 1969. The highlights included The Upsetters instrumental 'Return Of Django' US-301 making it to number 5 on the UK chart in 1969 with the instrumental featured on Trojan's first Reggae Chartbuster album. The label provided outlets for other artist including Bob Marley & The Wailers and Dave Barker. Some notable releases amongst quality recordings were 'Duppy Conqueror' US-348 and 'Small Axe' US-357 from Bob Marley & The Wailers and 'Well Dread' US-373 featuring Dennis Alcapone toasting over the rhythm of Eric Donaldson's 'Cherry Oh Baby'. The label would continue to release material until early 1973.

PYRAMID
(PREFIX) PRY

The original Pyramid label issued by Doctor Bird group included Desmond Dekker's 'Israelites' PRY-6058 and 'It Miek' PRY-6078 amongst its output. Trojan later revived the label after Doctor Bird had gone into liquidation.

ISLAND
(PREFIX) WIP

Chris Blackwell and Graeme Goodall had established Island as an outlet for Jamaican music in the UK as far back as 1959 with the company relocating to the UK in 1962. Without doubt the labels greatest asset was with Chris Blackwell's close friend Bob Marley who went onto become a worldwide superstar after the golden age of reggae had declined. Jimmy Cliff scored chart success with Island in 1970 with his version of a Cat Stevens penned song 'Wild World' WIP-6087 reaching number 8 in September that year. Island were also responsible for bringing reggae to the world stage with the soundtrack from the Jamaican feature film 'The Harder They Come' released on Island Records ILPS 9202 in 1972. At a time when the days were numbered for Trojan and Pama Chris Blackwell and Island were about to launch a reggae superstar, one that would inspire new life into reggae during the mid seventies, one that would become a true legend.

THE HISTORY OF SKINHEAD REGGAE 1968-1972   THE LABELS

BAMBOO RECORDS
(PREFIX) BAM

Junior Lincoln moved to North London in the early 60s at a time when very little Jamaican music was available, although artist such as Laurel Aitken and Jackie Edwards were performing live at venues in the capital. Ska had emerged as the dominant force in Jamaica during the early 60s and music was an essential element of life for the West Indians now living in England.

After a brief spell with Trojan Junior Lincoln set up his own Bamboo label from a shop at 88 Stroud Green in North London, 'Juniors Music Shop'. The shop was always packed at weekends with his customers eager for the latest tunes that Junior always seemed to get hold of. Singles were released on the Bamboo label with the prefix BAM along with albums between 1969 and 1972.

The records were licensed in the main from Clement Coxone Dodd with some self produced. Subsidiary labels of Bamboo were launched releasing a range of material on Ackee and Banana with the most notable releases on Bamboo coming from Bob & Marcia, Ken Booth, The Heptones, The Maytals and The Ethiopians.

CBS
(PREFIX) CBS

Reggae released on CBS came toward the end of the era when the pop influenced sound was clearly established. Paul Simon went to Jamaica to record 'Mother And Child Reunion' CBS S 793 to ensure he had an authentic reggae beat, travelling to the Dynamic Studios in Kingston. At the time he commented that "the equipment was so antiquated and falling apart and a take would have to be interrupted when goats would walk through the studio", but he did achieve that authentic feel. In essence that was what reggae was all about, down to earth no nonsense raw sounds, who needed sophisticated equipment. CBS were also responsible for the release of material from Johnny Nash who achieved chart success with his version of the Bob Marley penned 'Stir It Up' CBS 7800 peaking at number 13 in April 1972.

RHINO RECORDS
(PREFIX) RNO

Rhino Records was established at the end of the golden era in 1972 with the records manufactured and distributed by EMI. The label did enjoy chart success but it was with much sweetened versions of the real thing. The first release 'Mad About You' by Bruce Ruffin RNO-101 peaked at number 9 on the UK chart in July 1972. Desmond Dekker also released material on the label with 'Beware' RNO-107 issued late in 1972.

PAMA RECORDS

BULLET
(PREFIX) BU

Launched in 1969 the Bullet label released some high standard reggae featuring some good skinhead sounds amongst its quality output. Bullet was considered by many to be one of Pama's finest.

'Maga Dog' by Peter Tosh, 'Aily And Ailaloo' by Niney & Max, 'Rum Rhythm' from Roy Shirley, 'The Same Thing For Breakfast' Winston Groovy & Pat Rhoden along with 'Here Come The Heartaches' by Delroy Wilson are just a sample. They were fine offerings of the pure sound of reggae that had hardened from rocksteady. An album 'Bullet - A World Of Reggae' was issued on Pama SECO 19 during 1970.

CAMEL
(PREFIX) CU

Camel began with good quality productions and maintained the classic Pama reggae sound right through to the end of 72 with offerings from The Techniques 'Who You Gonna Run To', The Upsetters 'A Few Dollars More', The Uniques 'Watch This Sound' and 'Everybody Bawlin' by Dennis Alcapone & Lizzy. Add to those 'Linger A While' by John Holt, 'Nothing Can Separate Us' Owen Gray and the original 'Guilty' by Tiger and you have some of the finest recordings from the golden era of skinhead reggae.

CRAB
(PREFIX) CR

The Crab label was in production from 1968 through to 1971, seen as being Pama's most prolific label with the skinheads in mind, releasing the sound that appealed to the youth of the day. The list is never-ending with almost a third of the output credited to Derrick Morgan. The original 'Moon Hop' issued alongside such classic tracks as 'Send Me Some Loving', 'Hard Time', 'Take A Letter Maria' and 'Mek It Tan Deh', to name but a few. The Ethiopians came in with 'Reggae Hit The Town' with The Versatiles 'Children Get Ready', 'I Am King' and 'Spread Your Bed'.

Pama released several albums showcasing their labels during 1969-1970 on their budget ECO and SECO (Stereo) labels.

BULLET A WORLD OF REGGAE SECO-19 Released 1970

BU 399 Throw Me Corn - Winston Shan And The Sheiks 1969
BU 402 Heart Don't Leap - Dennis Walks 1969
BU 419 Copy Cats – The Clan 1970
BU 420 Each Time – The Ebony Sisters 1970
BU 425 Come By Here – Winston And Rupert 1970
BU 413 What's Your Excuse - The Hippy Boys 1969
BU 426 Theme From 'A Summer Place' – Ranny Williams 1970
BU 409 I Am Just A Minstrel - The Kingstonians 1969
BU 408 Love Of My Life - Dennis Walks 1969
BU 412 Hog In A Me Minti - The Hippy Boys 1969
BU 422 That's My Life (Because You Lied) – Fitzroy Sterling 1970
BU 401 Let Me Tell You Boy - Ebony Sisters 1969

THE BEST OF CAMEL SECO-18 Released 1970

CA 16 Strange Whispering - The West Indians 1969
CA 10 Who You Gonna Run To? - The Techniques 1969
CA 25 Girl What You're Doing To Me - Owen Grey 1969
CA 31 The Warrior – Johnny And The Sensations 1969
CA 30 Confidential - Lloyd Charmers 1969
CA 36 Bongo Nyah - The Little Roys 1969
CA 37 Every Beat Of My Heart – Owen Gray 1969
CA 40 In This World – The Federals 1970
CA 19B Go Find Yourself A Fool - The Techniques 1969
CA 14 Danny Boy – King Cannon 1969
CA 20 Since You Been Gone - Eric Fratter 1969
CA 23 Your Sweet Love - The Soul Cats 1969

ESCORT
(PREFIX) ES

Perhaps one of Pama's lesser known labels albeit with a handful of gems and one oddity. ES-824 was a release of 'Young Gifted And Black' by Bob Andy And Marcia Griffiths minus the strings that were such a prominent feature on the simultaneously released Trojan single, a record that was enjoying chart success. The oddity was more in the fact that Pama also released another version again on ES-824 'Young Gifted And Black' by Denzil And Jennifer replacing their Bob And Marcia version. Some of the gems were 'Man From Carolina', GG Allstars, 'Elizabethan Serenade' by Sweet Confusion and 'What Am I To Do' from Tony Scott.

GAS
(PREFIX) GAS

Gas was launched in 1968 following in the footsteps of Unity, Nu-Beat and Crab. The label seemed to lack direction, without doubt not the case with its forerunners. The label turned out several Bunny Lee productions, unusual as Lee already had his Unity label. The label released upward of seventy singles between 1968 and 1971.

NU-BEAT
(PREFIX NB

Following Pama's success from late 1967 through to early 1968 their first subsidiary label Nu-Beat was launched to promote Jamaican releases. Dandy approached Pama with a view to issuing his work on Nu-beat but the newly emerging Trojan offered Dandy his own Downtown label. One single did feature Dandy, 'Engine 59' NB-005. By 1969 Nu-Beat had become an outlet for Laurel Aitken with a change of policy to releasing UK productions and a change of name to Newbeat. Pama's version of 'Monkey Spanner' was released on NB-080. An Album of the labels best work was issued on Pama ECO 6 'Nu-Beats Greatest Hits' during 1969 featuring artists Max Romeo, Derrick Morgan, Alton Ellis and Laurel Aitken. Production on the label ceased in 1971.

GAS GREATEST HITS   ECO-4 Released 1969

GAS 112 1,000 Tons Of Megaton - Roland Alphonso 1969
GAS 115 How Long Will It Take - Pat Kelly 1969
GAS 103 Reggae In The Wind - Lester Sterling 1969
GAS 114 Walking Proud - Martin Riley 1969
GAS 117 Ain't Too Proud To Beg - The Uniques 1969
GAS 100 The Horse - Eric Barnett 1969
GAS 113 Soul Call - The Soul Rhythms 1969
GAS 118 Wanted - Baba Dise (Pama Dice) 1969
GAS 110B Never Give Up - Pat Kelly 1969
GAS 106 Te Ta Toe - Eric Barnett 1969
GAS 108 Ring Of Gold - The Melodians 1969
GAS 109 Cho Cho Train - Soul Cats 1969

NU-BEAT's GREATEST HITS   ECO-6 Released 1969

NB 014 La La Means I Love You - Alton Ellis 1968
NB 029 Rescue Me - The Reggae Girls 1969
NB 026 Another Heartache – Gregory Isaacs 1969
NB 019 Rhythm Hips - Ronald Russell 1968
NB 032 Haile Selassie - Laurel Aitken 1969
NB 031 My Testimony - The Maytals 1969
NB 001 Train To South Vietnam - The Rudies 1968
NB 008 Hey Boy, Hey Girl - Derrick And Patsy 1968
NB 022 Blowing In The Wind - Max Romeo 1969
NB 007 Rhythm And Soul - The Caltone All Stars 1968
NB 025 Suffering Still - Laurel Aitken 1969
NB 027B Give You My Love - Derrick & Paulette 1969

OCEAN
(PREFIX) OC

One of the last to be set up by Pama releasing less than ten singles perhaps the only one of note being the reissue from Unity of UN-503 Max Romeo's 'Wet Dream' from 1968.

PAMA
(PREFIX) PM

Pama's second release on the home label was 'What Will Your Mama Say' by Clancy Eccles PM-701, a record that enjoyed healthy sales and a few airings on radio one. The recordings came thick and fast including Lloyd Tyrell's (actually Lloyd Chalmers) suggestive 'Bang Bang Lulu' PM-710. Over one hundred and fifty singles were released on the Pama label up to the end of 1972. Gems included PM-835 'Way Down South' U. Roy and PM-856 'Good Hearted Woman' by The Clarendonians. One single that was never going to receive airplay was 'Sex Education' by The Classics PM-830 produced by Harry Palmer in 1971, it was however always a favourite at the school disco.

PAMA SUPREME
(PREFIX) PS

One of the last Pama labels to be set up it was seen as Pama's commercial label working with established artists in the UK. At the time it was described as Pama's version of Trojan, lots of strings and things. The labels biggest seller by far was Max Romeo's 'Let The Power Fall' PS-306, Denzil Dennis with 'South Of The Border' PS-350 and Cynthia Richards Jamaican offering 'Mr Postman' PS-366. At this time Trojan were issuing reggae version of pop hits recorded in Jamaica and Pama would issue a cover version of their own, usually less commercial, although Trojan inevitably had the upper hand.

CRAB BIGGEST HITS ECO 2 Released 1969

CRAB 9 Private Number - Ernest Wilson 1969
CRAB 10 Run Girl Run - G.G. Grossett 1969
CRAB 2 Fire A Muss Muss Tail - The Ethiopians 1969
CRAB 1 Children Get Ready - The Versatiles 1969
CRAB 8 Seven Letters - Derrick Morgan 1969
CRAB 4 Reggae Hit The Town - The Ethiopians 1969
CRAB 12 Work It - The Viceroys 1969
CRAB 3 River To The Bank - Derrick Morgan 1969
CRAB 5 Spread Your Bed - The Versatiles 1969
CRAB 7B What A Big Surprise - The Ethiopians 1969
CRAB 6 Reggae City - Val Bennett 1969
CRAB 8B Lonely Heartaches - The Tartans (The Clarendonians) 1969

REGGAE HITS '69 ECO 3 Released 1969 a selection of tracks from various labels.

CRAB 1   Children Get Ready – The Versatiles 1968
UN 502   Bangarang – Lester Sterling 1968
NB 008   Hey Boy Hey Girl – Derrick Morgan 1968
NB 019   Rhythm Hips – Ronald Russell 1968
CRAB 3   River To The Bank – Derrick Morgan 1968
CRAB 4   Reggae Hit The Town – The Ethiopians 1968
GAS 100   The Horse – Eric Barnett 1968
NB 016   I Love You – Derrick Morgan 1968
GAS 103   Reggae In The Wind – Lester Sterling 1968
NB 021   Let's Have Some Fun – Devon And The Tartans 1969
NB 017   Push Push – The Termites 1968
UN 501   Last Flight To Reggae City – Tommy McCook Cole 1968

PUNCH
(PREFIX) PH

A label does not make a record great but in the case of Punch it gave a clearly defined image with a fist smashing into a 1969 top 20 chart. A favourite with the skinheads the early releases concentrated on skinhead reggae from Lee 'Scratch' Perry with the official follow up to his UK hit single 'Return Of Django', 'Clint Eastwood' released on PH-21. The record just failed to chart but not due to its popularity with the skinheads more down to poor distribution, a decision that Perry admitted he had got wrong leasing the track to Pama. Perry released several strong selling singles notably 'Return Of The Ugly' PH-18 and 'Dry Acid' PH-19 both bought in great numbers by the West Indian community and the skinheads. Confusion was often in evidence when it came to Pama releases and one such incident fell around Dave Barker's 'Shocks Of Mighty', released on Punch PH-25 and Trojan's Upsetter label at the same time, with Barker said to have been unaware of the Pama release. Other notable releases included 'Cherrio Baby' by The Classics PH-79 and 'Johnny Too Bad' by The Slickers PH-59 a track also released on Trojan's Dynamic label. Strange as it was a release of Punch's greatest hits was never forthcoming.

SUPREME
(PREFIX) SUP

The label only issued twenty nine singles during its short rein from 1969 to 1971. One that stands out is Bob Marley's 'I Like It Like This' AKA 'Don't Rock My Boat' released on SUP-216.

UNITY
(PREFIX) UN

The label was set up to provide Pama with a solid link to a Jamaican producer, Bunny Lee, who could supply the label with a constant succession of quality Jamaican hits. This was seen as a long term venture with Pama paying for the records to be recorded in Jamaica. 'Bangarang' UN-502 by Stranger Cole and Lester Sterling would prove very successful, a new sound having a jerky organ line cited by many as to be the first authentic reggae record. Bunny Lee began issuing records in Jamaica using the same Unity design with the label becoming synonymous with Bunny Lee productions. The fourth release on the label was Lee's production of Max Romeo's legendary 'Wet Dream' UN-503 using Derrick Morgan's 'Hold You Jack' rhythm track. The record remained on the UK chart for an incredible six months despite its ban by the BBC. The end for Unity was set in motion when Lee began licensing work to Trojan's Jackpot label in 1970.

THE HISTORY OF SKINHEAD REGGAE 1968-1972   THE LABELS

PUNCH SELECTED DISCOGRAPHY
Strange as it was a release of Punch's greatest hits was never forthcoming.

PH 01 The Burner - The Dynamics 1969
PH 02 Mix Up Girl - The Creation 1969
PH 19 Dry Acid - The Upsetters 1969
PH 21 Clint Eastwood - The Upsetters 1969
PH 23 Ram You Hard - The Bleechers 1969
PH 25 Shock Of Mighty - Dave Barker 1969
PH 35 Serious - Maytones 1970
PH 55 Hold The Ghost - Herman 1971
PH 65 Cholera - The Justins 1971
PH 102 Lively Up Yourself - Bob Marley And The Wailers 1972
PH 104 Nanny Skank - U Roy 1972
PH 108 A Sugar - Roy Shirley 1972

UNITY'S GREATEST HITS ECO 7 Released 1969

UN 502 Bangarang - Lester Sterling & Stranger Cole 1968
UN 501 Last Flight To Reggae City - Tommy McCook 1968
UN 513 Let It Be Me - Slim Smith & Paulette 1969
UN 504 Everybody Needs Love - Slim Smith 1968
UN 505 Reggae On Broadway - Lester Sterling 1969
UN 511 Twelfth Of Never – Max Romeo (actually Pat Kelly) 1969
UN 509 Spoogy - Lester Sterling 1969
UN 508 For Once In My Life - Slim Smith 1969
UN 502B If We Should Ever Meet - Stranger Cole 1968
UN 506 The Avengers - Tommy McCook 1969
UN 500 On Broadway - Slim Smith 1968
UN 512B Bright As A Rose - Lester Sterling 1969

A MUSICIANS TALE

Ian 'Smithy' Smith recalls his memories of reggae as a musician during the skinhead years.

"I joined an existing group as keyboard player, aged 18, in 1966. By 1968 the group's name (back then, they were called 'groups'; 'bands' were either Brass or Big Bands - and they played instruments and didn't just sing, look pretty and dance around!) had changed from The Inner Circle to The Inner Mind and our music had also changed from Atlantic Records-style soul, Small Faces, Spencer Davis Group stuff to include rocksteady, as it was known then, and reggae.

This was due to the boss of the Huddersfield West Indian Association, Errol Babb, bringing me seven records he wanted us to play at a forthcoming West Indian Dance. We were the only white people there on the night & when we featured these rocksteady tracks, the crowd went wild. That was that, as far as we were concerned until 6 weeks later, we were appearing at Sheffield's Shades Club, I heard the D.J. playing one of the tracks we'd learned, Prince Buster's 'Shaking up Orange Street', so we reintroduced the songs into the act and, yep, the crowd went wild again! From that moment onwards, The Inner Mind became well known at most of the West Indian centres in the country – London's Apollo and Q(Cue) Club, Bristol's Bamboo, Club 67 at Wolverhampton and Santa Rosa, Birmingham, Bobby's in Mosside, Manchester, Leeds International Club, Huddersfield's Venn Street, Arawak, Shalimar and Fartown International Clubs etc.

It was somewhat of a strange coincidence that we ended up recording for Pama Records. Basically, besides our own show, over the months we'd backed Laurel Aitken (a lot), Owen Gray (several times), Winston Groovy (twice) & Alton Ellis, so Pama had heard of us and our reputation. We'd done a gig in High Wycombe with Owen & on the following night, we'd taken a gig at Pama's Apollo Club in Harlesden - just The Inner Mind. When we got there, there seemed to be a sort of strange atmosphere and the boss (Jeff Palmer) started getting awkward with me. We set up our gear and then he said he wasn't going to pay us our full fee, no reason given. It was obvious he was just 'trying it on'; as we were down there from Yorkshire, reluctantly I said OK, we'll take the reduction; ten minutes later, he tried it on again saying he would pay us less. At that, the Yorkshire white reggae band said 'Stuff you', packed up and went north! That night, the Apollo ended up without an act or, at best, a last minute replacement. This was our first dealings with a Palmer brother and in hindsight - nothing really changed.

Don Auty was one of the employees at Pama's artiste's agency called 'Apollo Artists'. Don was, even then, an old-school theatrical agent, originally from Dewsbury/Batley in Yorkshire, who ended up firstly in the West End and then rather down-market in Harlesden. He persuaded us to give it one more try and we became a regular at the Apollo, on an agreed fee and billed as 'The Greatest White Reggae Band on Earth'.

Somewhat of a change of heart on Jeff Palmer's part! We began giving some of our recordings to Pama for release. Jeff even took us all out to a restaurant after a gig at the club to offer us a job as one of Pama's resident studio bands, alongside The Mohawks and, to a lesser extent The Rudies, but we declined. Surprise, surprise the money offered was absolutely dire & it would mean moving to London, which none of us wanted, and relying on Apollo Artists for most of our gigs, a bit iffy, to say the least, so we probably made the right decision. One act, we found out later, got gigs in Italy & had to sell their gear to get back home; whether that was due to the agency or the promoter was never made clear, but the result was the same. Back then the gigs were a great experience - it was a completely underground scene; the music press looked down on the reggae market, university students hadn't started to pretend to like it yet and mainstream radio would have rather broadcast a political rant by Tony Benn, especially the BBC, than play a reggae record. It was a completely alien concept! We hardly ever played white venues during this period; universities stopped booking us (we weren't progressive rock etc.), dance clubs - er, discos – couldn't dance to us but we were on cloud nine at the gigs we did! Our records which were released under our own name or as backings for other artists were just boosters for our reputation at the live gigs. We, as countless others, never got paid for the records we made.

During the skinhead years, we had records out on Pama's NewBeat & Bullet labels under our own name. They also released a track called 'Breakdown Rock' on Pama Supreme Records as The Harlesden Monk; this was actually 'Dreams of Yesterday' by The Inner Mind, released on Shades Records! which brings me to 'Pum Pum Girl' on NewBeat Records. We'd done some backing tracks for Laurel Aitken at a studio down in London and at that session, we'd also done 'Witchcraft Man', destined to be our first single on Pama's NewBeat label. I'd given Laurel an acetate of eight tracks we'd recorded at 'Mat' Mathias' King Street Studios in Huddersfield for the Shades label in Sheffield. 'Dreams' was released on Shades, followed up by 'Jesse James Hits Back'. In the meantime, Pama slipped out 'Pum Pum Girl', one of the above mentioned tracks on NewBeat, produced by me not Laurel Aitken as the label wrongly stated. They'd pressed it up from that copy of the acetate and had not used the original tape, cos of course they didn't have it. Max Omare, at Shades, made them withdraw the single, and so potentially stopped the record being a massive seller although we probably wouldn't have got paid anyway! When 'Dreams' was snuck out as 'Breakdown Rock' it was no surprise. And that's why I set up Hot Lead Records and Castle Hill Music, to safeguard all my songs, productions & recordings.

Just a footnote, 'Pum Pum Girl' was the 'Dreams of Yesterday' backing track with suggestive words added. I lived in Thornhill Lees, Dewsbury at the time; I caught the bus to Huddersfield one night to get to Mat's two track recording studio, nothing posh, just primitive, simple and great. I wrote the lyrics on the bus on the way there! So, had the mood taken me, it could've ended up a sentimental love song!"

TELL IT LIKE IT WAS

Ian continued to say "*I did write some love songs but, for some reason, 'Pum Pum Girl' and more so 'Doggie Bite Postman as 'Smithy All Stars', our biggest seller, were to be my legacy! Those days were, to me, golden days, an underground scene of music we loved, endless recording sessions & gigs, much merriment and booze, it couldn't last. The spoken intro to 'Dreams' which was spliced off the Pama Supreme PS352 release says it all. 'I remember how it used to be, the pattern of time moves on regardless'. That's far too philosophical for reggae - no wonder they cut it off the record! Reggae is fun, sun and rum! I'm still at it, much older, no wiser but doing the odd gig with the old Inner Mind members, Jimmy Walsh (Drums) and Dave Tattersall (Bass)."*

Throughout Britain the story of how skinheads and reggae became intertwined has been told time and time again by many, all reiterating that the original skinheads were non racist and had no interest in politics, most coming from working class backgrounds. All reggae between 1968 -1972 can be classed as skinhead reggae, but what influence did the skinheads have in the development of the Jamaican music scene. The buying power of the youth had created an international audience away from Jamaica for the first time. The skinheads began to buy reggae at a rate not seen before outside of the island, and some records were now selling in sufficient quantities to begin charting in the UK, an event that would force the hand of the BBC to add the skinhead sounds to their restrictive playlists. 'Wet Dream' had sold over 250,000 copies despite its ban and was ranked 51 in the top selling singles of 1969.

I recall my first encounter with the incessant rhythm of Jamaican music, at the school disco, '007 Shanty Town' would have been amongst the first, and on hearing the risqué but melodic Wet Dream I gathered together all the change I could and hurried to the local record store. My first purchase, a shiny vinyl single, released on what was to me at the time the obscure Unity label for about five bob. The sad thing was though I never had a record player to play it on, but my best mate Richard did, a posh stereogram, and it was played over and over again. Richard I recall also built up a good collection of Trojan albums. In those early days with no radio exposure discovering the new sounds from Jamaica was always an exciting challenge.

Chris Brown author of the skinhead book 'Booted & Suited' recalls the golden days in Bristol at a place I also have fond memories of hanging about on a Saturday.
"*If you wanted to buy your vinyl records there was a very well known shop on Picton Street called RCA records. That stood for Record Collectors Association. It was run by a guy called Ray and his dad. It was really the only place you could get West Indian music or soul music. Even then you wouldn't know the records because you couldn't hear this music at all, a lot of it was word of mouth. You would go down on the Saturday morning and they would just play music and you would try and buy it, I say try and buy it because a lot of people would say, "I'll have that one," and the RCA might only have one copy of it. It was a great little shop, full, absolutely jam packed with albums and singles.*

It just had a great vibe in there and was a really nice place to hang around on a Saturday and buy music".

The early development of West Indian music in Britain can be traced back to June 1948 when The Empire Windrush docked at Tilbury, carrying 493 passengers from Jamaica, wishing to start a new life in the United Kingdom. Virgil Jack Williams recalls his arrival in Britain two decades later.

"I arrived in a cold damp London in 1962 having spent my early years growing up bathed by the warmth of the sun blessed West Indies, where blue beat, calypso and mento music always seemed to fill the balmy nights. In London at that time I was not allowed to soak up the nightlife in the pubs as all had banned entry with notices stating 'NO COLOURED OR IRISH' allowed.

Music was an inherent part of the West Indian culture and we would go to big dance hall events in West London, not far from where I was living at the time in Edgware Road. The dance halls were popular venues although no food was served, just drinks and a generous helping of great music, a combination of steel bands, calypso and ska. I recall with fond memories one evening we had a visit from Cassius Clay, around the time of the great Cooper fight, his appearance caused a real stir and great interest. I was now living with a black family in London and although it was difficult to get hold of we did manage to come by some blue beat and ska records imported from Jamaica. The music was beginning to become more prevalent as the decade went on with ska now being played at the Hammersmith Palais and other clubs such as 'Burtons', a hot spot, and on one occasion Pan's People came to dance.

After the clubs we would go onto 'Blues Parties' often held in someone's house where a large sound system would be pumping out ska and rocksteady into the night, you didn't need to know the address you just had to follow the sound of incessant rhythms booming out. The MC would 'toast' over the music as the drink and food flowed freely including traditional rice peas, jerk chicken and red stripe, with the venues always packed. The opportunity to buy West Indian music was still very limited, and little if any was played on national radio, so the clubs and impromptu parties with their sound systems allowed us to soak up the music with all of our friends.

Towards the end of the decade record shops began to open specialising in the imported hits from Jamaica and would always be crowded on a Saturday, with everyone anxious to hear the latest tunes from back home. The youth both white and black with their cropped hair who rejected the hippie attitude and progressive music took an interest in reggae; much like their elder brothers did with ska earlier in the decade. Add to this mix the birth of record labels in the UK and soon reggae had found its rightful international acclaim. With the sound from the islands available to the mainstream record buying public for the first time, reggae was now charting".

YOU CAN GET IT IF YOU REALLY WANT
TROJAN RECORDS TBL 146
Released 1970

DESMOND DEKKER AND THE ACES

Desmond Dacres was born in 1941 in the parish of St Andrew Jamaica, moving to Kingston as a boy. Desmond worked as a welder but always had a passion for music. In time after a couple of failed attempts, being rejected first by Dodd then Duke Reid, Desmond eventually got an audition at Beverley's Studio. Following the audition Leslie Kong quickly arranged his first recording at Federal Studios, 'Honour Your Mother And Father' giving Desmond his first hit.

A succession of hits in Jamaica and good sales in England followed including his 1966 rocksteady recording '007', a song about the troubles in Jamaica, making reference to James Bond and Ocean's 11. The record, with Desmond accompanied by The Aces, reached number 14 in the UK during July 1967, and also charted on the other side of the Atlantic.

It was however in 1968 that Desmond's biggest UK hit, one of the early up-and-coming reggae sounds '(Poor Mi) Israelites' was released, and following steady sales over a long period it eventually entered the UK charts in March 1969, before peaking at number 1 in April.

'Israelites' was the first reggae record to achieve the number 1 spot on the 19th April 1969 where it spent just a week before being replaced with 'Get Back' by the Beatles, a record that came straight into the coveted spot. 'Israelites' remained on the charts for a total of fifteen weeks during 1969 and would make several forays back into the charts with subsequent re issues over the next couple of decades.

The Beatles supposedly made reference to Desmond in a song penned by Paul McCartney 'Ob-La-Di, Ob-La-Da'. Sadly Desmond died of a heart attack in May 2006 at the age of 64 but not before leaving behind a lasting legacy by way of a tremendous amount of excellent recordings. Some of which were to provide further chart success in the UK before the end of 1972, most notably the Jimmy Cliff penned song 'You Can Get It If You Really Want' a record that would later feature as the opening song to Perry Henzell's accomplished 1972 cult film, 'The Harder They Come' although sung by Cliff himself.

ISRAELITES   DESMOND DEKKER AND THE ACES
Released on PYRAMID PYR 6058 1968
Highest chart position 1 19/04/1969

The other popular sounds around when Desmond was on the top spot provide quite a mix in musical style.

1. **Desmond Dekker - Israelites.**
2. Mary Hopkin. - Goodbye
3. Marvin Gaye - I Heard It Through The Grapevine
4. Lulu - Boom Bang -A- Bang
5. Dean Martin - Gentle On My Mind
6. The Who - Pinball Wizard
7. The Hollies - Sorry Suzanne
8. The Foundations - In The Bad Old Days
9. Joe South - Games People Play
10. Noel Harrison - The Windmills Of Your Mind

Israelites riding high in the UK charts had signalled the beginning of period of great success for Desmond who by this time had established a special artist / producer relationship with Leslie Kong. Kong as we will discover was to become the most successful producer of the late sixties through to the very early seventies creating a distinctive sound, combining an infectious commercial appeal whilst preserving the Jamaican sound that was great to dance to.

Further chart success followed 'Israelites' with a total change of style with 'It Miek' telling about his little sister. The record, a slightly different sound to the original Jamaican release was issued on the Pyramid label in 1969, as with Israelites the song was written by Desmond and Lesley Kong. 'It Miek' often spelt 'It Mek' entered the UK charts in 1969 spending eleven weeks in the top 50 peaking at number 7 for two weeks during July. Desmond's fourth chart success 'Pickney Gal' did not emulate the previous incursions into the lofty heights entering at number 42 in January 1970, its highest position, spending a mere three weeks in the top 50, nevertheless a record that ranks amongst his finest, rich with Jamaican patois lyrics.

'Pickney Gal' was the last of Desmond's recording to be released on the Pyramid label and the last featuring The Aces. Leslie Kong went on to form an association with the up and coming Trojan, a label that was enjoying considerable chart success with artists such as Jimmy Cliff, The Upsetters and The Pioneers to name but a few. Ironically it was Jimmy Cliff who penned Desmond's next success 'You Can Get It If You Really Want'. Entering the charts at number 46 in August 1970 where it would spend two weeks at number 2 during October that year.

YOU CAN GET IT IF YOU REALLY WANT   DESMOND DEKKER
Released on TROJAN TR-7777   1970
Highest chart position   2   10/10/1970

The gulf in musical syle was quite extreme comparing Desmond's vibrant sound to Deep Purple and Balck Sabbath.

1. Freda Payne - Band Of Gold
2. **Desmond Dekker - You Can Get It If You Really Want**
3. Deep Purple - Black Night
4. Black Sabbath - Paranoid
5. Bobby Bloom - Montego Bay
6. The Carpenters - (They Long To Be) Close To You
7. Diana Ross - Ain't No Mountain High Enough
8. The Tremeloes - Me And My Life
9. Chairman Of The Board - Give Me Just A Little More Time
10. Poppy Family Featuring Susan Jacks - Which Way You Goin' Billy

After the success of 'You Can Get It If You Really Want' Desmond recorded numerous tracks but only released a couple more singles, none enjoying the previous chart success. Leslie Kong had become Desmond's mentor with unrivalled chart success continuing until his untimely death in 1971, when Kong died of a heart attack at the relatively young age of 38. His death was to have a shattering effect on Desmond, and it has been said, perhaps one that he never fully recovered from in terms of his music.

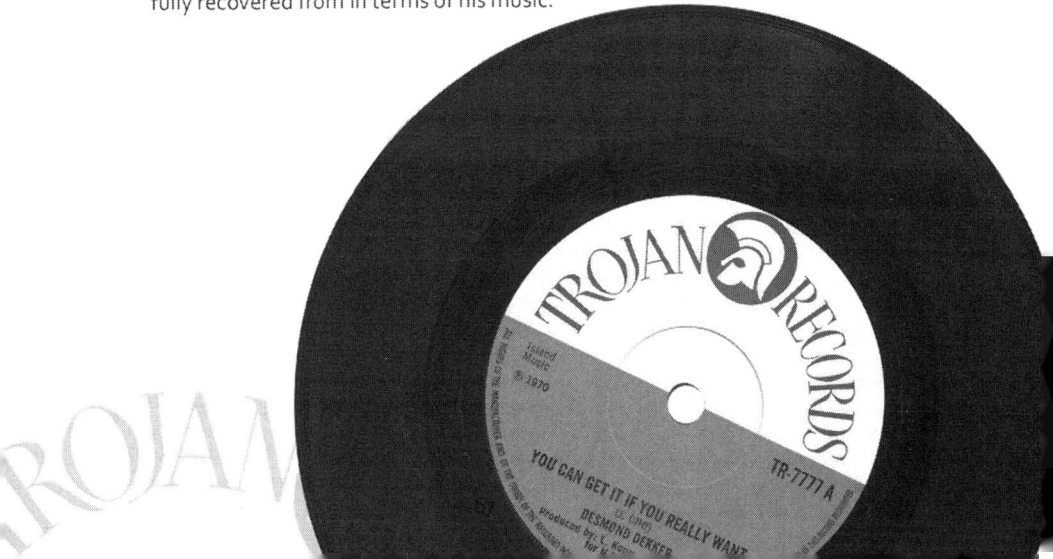

YOU CAN GET IT IF YOU REALLY WANT
TROJAN RECORDS TBL 146   Released 1970

Side 1
1. YOU CAN GET IT IF YOU REALLY WANT
2. I BELIEVE
3. PERSEVERANCE
4. GET UP LITTLE SUZIE
5. PEACE ON THE LAND
6. CINDY

Side 2
1. PICKNEY GAL
2. YOU GOT SOUL
3. COOMYAH
4. THAT'S THE WAY LIFE GOES
5. PEACE OF MIND
6. POLKA DOT

DISCOGRAPHY SINGLES 1968 - 1972

PYRAMID

DESMOND DEKKER AND THE ACES

PYR-6020 Sabotage 1968
PYR-6031 Beautiful And Dangerous 1968
PYR-6044 Mother Pepper 1968
PYR-6051 Intensified '68 1968
PYR-6058 (Poor Mi) Israelites 1968
PYR-6058 It Mek 1969
PYR-6068 Problems 1969
PYR-6078 Pickney Gal 1969

TROJAN

DESMOND DEKKER

TR-7777 You Can Get It If You Really Want 1970
TR-7802 The Song We Used To Sing 1970
TR-7847 Licking Stick 1971
TR-7847 Live And Learn 1971
TR-7876 It Gotta Be So 1972

RHINO

DESMOND DEKKER

RNO-107 Beware 1972

DISCOGRAPHY ALBUMS 1968-1972

THIS IS DESMOND DEKKAR
TROJAN RECORDS TTL 4 (Leslie Kong) 1969

YOU CAN GET IT IF YOU REALLY WANT
TROJAN RECORDS TBL 146 (Leslie Kong) 1970

MAX ROMEO

Max Romeo was born Maxwell Livingstone Smith, in the parish of St Anne, on the north coast of Jamaica in 1944. Max endured hardship in his early years, moving to Kingston at the age of 10, then leaving home at 14. Max's first introduction to the record industry came after a spell labouring on a sugar plantation finding himself delivering records, always singing as he went. His potential was soon spotted and he was advised to enter a talent contest, a move that was to see him head back to Kingston in search of fame and fortune.

Max's first record was released in 1967 titled 'I'll Buy You A Rainbow' with a group called the Emotions with Max as the lead singer. The single made number 2 in Jamaica and established Max as a star.

A move that would eventually bring worldwide fame for Max was an introduction to Derrick Morgan's brother in law, producer Bunny Lee, who was trialling with the new sound evolving as reggae. Bunny 'Striker' Lee would later persuaded Max to go solo.

The name Romeo is said to have come about due to Max spending time with a girl. The story goes that Max was talking to the girl at eight in the morning when her father left for work. Max returned to see the girl later in the day just a short time before her father returned from work. Thinking Max had been there all day, stood in the same spot, the father said to Max, 'You must be Romeo'. Bunny Lee heard the story and recommended that Max should change his stage name to Max Romeo.

Max began writing songs and Bunny Lee came to Max with a suggestion for doing a rude song, a theme that was becoming popular with some of the other artists at the time. Max penned 'Wet Dream' but history tells that he did not want to perform it. Lee wanted Derrick Morgan to record the song who had previously released 'Hold You Jack' also penned by Max Romeo using the same rhythm. Derrick refused so Bunny, after declines by others including John Holt, persuaded Max to voice the lyrics.

THE HISTORY OF SKINHEAD REGGAE 1968-1972   MAX ROMEO

Max has been quoted as saying that he was forced to do that song by Bunny Lee. He claimed he was actually threatened, being told if he did not do the song he could not stay around. Several versions of this story have been told but what is in no doubt the song became a huge hit in Jamaica.

The song was eventually sent over to England with a batch of other recordings to Pama who subsequently released it on their Unity label in 1968 and the rest as they say is history, lie dung gal......................

The record managed an airing or two courtesy of Emperor Rosko on Radio One before the hierarchy got wind of the patois content. Max claimed that the song was telling the story of his leaking roof but the BBC were having none of it, describing it as bawdy, and immediately censored the record. The ban did however serve to make it more popular with the new skinheads who were beginning their love affair with the raw sounds of the new rhythms originating from Jamaica.

The record took the charts by storm in May 1969 despite having no further air play on the BBC. The record was always referred to as "a record by Max Romeo" during a rundown of the charts. It eventually made it into the top thirty reaching number 10 in August 1969 and was reported to have sold over 250,000 copies, the record spending a very respectful twenty five weeks on the charts.

The chart speaks for itself in highlighting what a massive contrast 'Wet Dream' was in comparison to the rest of the top ten, and how the skinheads would have warmed to the incessant rhythm, a sound they would claim for their own, along that was with their West Indian friends.

During August 1969 at the top of the pile were the Rolling Stones with quite a variety of musical style between them and Max at number 10.

WET DREAM   MAX ROMEO
Released on UNITY UN-503   1968
Highest chart position   10   16/08/1969

1. Rolling Stones – Honkey Tonk Woman
2. Robin Gibb – Saved By The Bell
3. Joe Dolan – Make Me An Island
4. Plastic Ono Band – Give Peace A Chance
5. Stevie Wonder – My Cherie Amour
6. Clodagh Rodgers – Goodnight Midnight
7. Cilla Black – Conversations
8. Vanity Fare – Early In The Morning
9. Love Affair – Bring Back The Good Times
10. **Max Romeo – Wet Dream**

A tour of the UK followed with the subsequent release of the album, 'A Dream', issued by Pama. Although Max was banned from performing at several venues many did allow him on stage, with Max remaining in England for eighteen months. A follow up single again on Unity,' Mini Skirt Vision' failed to enter the charts but the rude image was destined to stay with him for a long while, however on his return to Jamaica Max was determined to change musical direction.

THE HISTORY OF SKINHEAD REGGAE 1968-1972 MAX ROMEO

Max became increasingly aware of the social injustices in Jamaica and the huge gulf between the rich and the poor with his music reflecting the restlessness in his homeland. 'Let The Power Fall On I' in 1971 and 'Are You Sure', released on Pama Supreme in 1972 along with 'Pray For Me' released in 1972 on High Note and Pama Supreme labels were to represent the way forward for Max, showing that his musical talent went far beyond risqué lyrics.

PRAY FOR ME High Note HS-058 1972 and Pama Supreme PS-345 1972

'Let The Power Fall' was adopted by The Peoples National Party during the Jamaican General Election of 1972, a campaign that saw the late Michael Manley elected Prime Minister.

A DREAM   PAMA RECORDS   Released 1969   PAMA PMLP 11

Side 1
1. WET DREAM (electronically rebalanced)   2. A NO FEE ME PICKNEY
3. FAR FAR AWAY   4. THE HORN   5. HEAR MY PLEA   6. LOVE

Side 2
1. I DON'T WANT TO LOOSE YOUR LOVE   2. WOOD UNDER CELLAR
3. WHINE HER GOOSIE   4. CLUB RAID   5. YOU CAN'T STOP ME

SINGLES DISCOGRAPHY 1968 - 1972

UNITY
UN-503 Wet Dream   1968

ISLAND
WI-3111 Walk In The Dawn 1968
WI-3104 Put Me In The Mood   1968

BLUE CAT
BS-161 Me Want Man   1969
BS-163 It's Not The Way   1969

NU BEAT
NB-022 Blowing In The Wind   1969

UNITY
UN-507 Belly Woman   1969
UN-511 Twelfth Of Never   1969   (actually Pat Kelly)
UN-516 Wine Her Goosie   1969
UN-532 Mini-Skirt Vision   1969
UN-547 What A Cute Man   1970
UN-560 Fish In The Pot   1970

CAMEL
CA-82 The Coming Of Jah   1971

PAMA SUPREME
PS-306 Let The Power Fall   1971
PS-318 Don't You Weep   1971
PS-328 Ginal Ship   1971

UNITY
UN-571 Macabee Version   1971

CAMEL
CA-85 Rasta Band Wagon   1972
CA-86 Public Enemy Number One   1972

DYNAMIC
DYN-444 We Love Jamaica   1972

GG RECORDS
GG-4535 Is It Really Over   1972

THE PIONEERS

The Pioneers roots were originally formed way back in the days of blue-beat by brothers Sydney and Derrick Crooks with Winston Hewitt making up the trio releasing singles in Jamaica on the Caltone label. Glen Adams joined the group replacing Winston Hewitt but their output did not find success. This led to Sydney concentrating on promoting concerts and the original group disbanding in 1967.

In spite of this it would not be long before Sydney took a job at Joe Gibbs record shop, purchased by Gibbs originally as a TV repair shop, on Beeston Street in Kingston, the record sales proving successful leading to Joe's involvement in the music industry.

The story goes that Sydney wanted to record a duet so promptly enlisted the services of Jackie Robinson who was by trade a welder who just happened to be singing in the street. The song was 'Gimmie Little Loving' and sold well in their native Jamaica. A partnership was duly formed with Jackie taking the role as the lead singer.

Subsequent releases followed including 'Long Shot Bus Me Bet', a song about a race horse that was destined for fame, with the duo constantly riding high in the islands charts.

In late 1968 a third member joined to complete the trio, George Agard, who had previously enjoyed a solo career but his attributes worked well, resulting in one of the most popular groups in the history of Jamaican music being born. The Pioneers became a group that had a significant influence on the British charts and the youth of the day, the skinheads.

A change of producer came about with the group working for the up and coming Leslie Kong's Beverleys label. The trio's second recording was 'Long Shot Kick De Bucket' in 1969, a sequel to the earlier hit telling of the death of the famous race horse at Kingston's Caymanas Park. The song was to provide yet more chart success in Jamaica. Trojan took a gamble, not intended as a pun, releasing the record as they could see the potential for a hit. The record was however ignored by the BBC who refused to include it on their play list. 'Long Shot Kick De Bucket' was receiving airplay on independent stations and became popular in the clubs but without national exposure very few would hear the record.

The BBC finally gave in and added it to their play list in the autumn of 1969 with it entering the charts in October. The record peaked at a respectful number 21 in November and remained on the charts for eleven weeks. That was the first real introduction to The Pioneers for the skinheads who had by now developed a strong relationship to the music.

Included on the Trojan album TBL103 'Long Shot' released in 1969 were tracks in the same vein including 'Black Bud' and 'Poor Rameses'.

'Long Shot Kick The Bucket' is a tale of the weeping and wailing that ensued after 'Long Shot' was pulled up in the first race at Caymanas Park, Kingston Jamaica. The race was underway with Clearblade and Combat leading Corazon with Long Shot at the rear. It seems that Combat fell then Long Shot fell and as a consequence as they say, all their money they had bet had gone to hell.

Two more chart hits were to follow for Trojan and The Pioneers, albeit in a different vein to their original recordings with 'Let Your Yeah Be Yeah' reaching number 5 in September 1971 and 'Give And Take' only managing number 35 in January 1972.

'Let Your Yeah Be Yeah' went on to become the best selling reggae record of 1971, a celebration not held in high esteem by some who saw it as a diversification from pure reggae. To an extent it was but none the less worked very well allowing the music to interact with the mainstream but retaining its fundamental Jamaican feel, setting it apart from the other records of the day.

Both hits were penned by the up and coming Jimmy Cliff who became a prolific singer, song-writer and actor. Reggae was not however all about chart hits, yes it did bring the music to the fore but The Pioneers continued to produce a string of reggae 'hits' over the next couple of years. These were in direct contrast to the more raw down to earth sounds that were still being released by Pama, but were still none the less well received including, 'I need Your Sweet Inspiration' and 'Roll Muddy River'. As a consequence of this change of musical direction from The Pioneers original sounds, to the more pop influenced reggae, further chart success eluded them.

The Pioneers released some thirty singles during the golden age of reggae from 1968 through to the end of 1972.

THE HISTORY OF SKINHEAD REGGAE 1968-1972   THE PIONEERS

Stiff competition was running through the UK charts when The Pioneers 'Let Your Yeah Be Yeah' peaked at number 5 in September 1971.

The British charts of the 11th September 1971 looked like this:

1. Diana Ross – I'm Still Waiting
2. The Tams – Hey Girl Don't Bother Me
3. Dawn – What Are You Doing Sunday
4. The New Seekers – The Never Ending Song Of Love
5. **The Pioneers – Let Your Yeah Be Yeah**
6. Nancy Sinatra And Lee Hazelwood – Did You Ever
7. Buffy Sainte Marie – Soldier Blue
8. The Supremes – Nathan Jones
9. Curved Air – Back Street Luv
10. Carole King – It's Too Late / Feel The Earth Move

GREETINGS FROM THE PIONEERS
Released on Amalgamated   AMGLP-2003 1968

Side 1
1. ME NAW GO A BELIEVE   2. YOU WILL NEVER GET AWAY
3. BABY DON'T BE LATE   4. SHAKE IT UP   5. NO DOPE ME PONT
6. WHIP THEM

Side 2
1. GIMME GIMME GIRL   2. THINGS JUST GOT TO CHANGE
3. SWEET DREAMS   4. TICKLE ME FOR DAYS   5. JACKPOT
6. GIVE ME A LITTLE LOVING

THE HISTORY OF SKINHEAD REGGAE 1968-1972   THE PIONEERS

LONG SHOT   THE PIONEERS   TROJAN RECORDS TBL103
Released 1969

LONG SHOT

Produced by: Leslie Kong.
All tracks written by: Agard, Crooks, Robinson

Side 1
1. LONG SHOT KICK DE BUCKET   2. CARANAPO   3. BLACK BUD
4. LONG UP YOUR MOUTH   5. BRING HIM COME   6. MOTHER RITTY

Side 2
1. POOR RAMESES   2. SAMFIE MAN   3. BELLY GUT   4. LUCKY SIDE
5. TROUBLE DE A BUSH   6. BOSS FESTIVAL

With 'Long Shot Kick De Bucket' heading up the British charts the trio flew to England to promote the record on an initial six week tour. The Pioneers had by now recorded several of their own penned songs for Leslie Kong back in Jamaica, tracks that would feature on their second album 'Long Shot'.

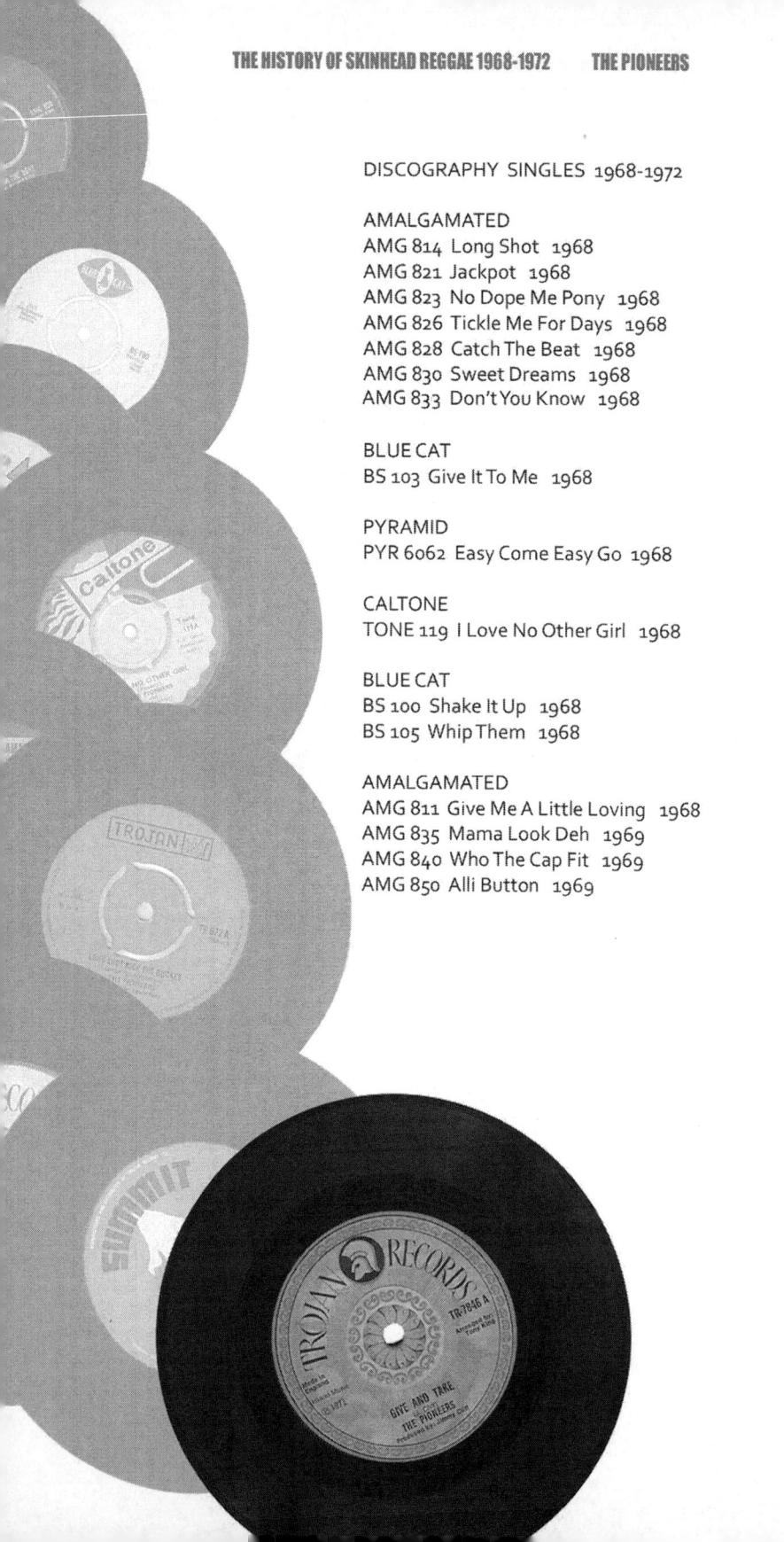

THE HISTORY OF SKINHEAD REGGAE 1968-1972   THE PIONEERS

DISCOGRAPHY SINGLES 1968-1972

AMALGAMATED
AMG 814 Long Shot 1968
AMG 821 Jackpot 1968
AMG 823 No Dope Me Pony 1968
AMG 826 Tickle Me For Days 1968
AMG 828 Catch The Beat 1968
AMG 830 Sweet Dreams 1968
AMG 833 Don't You Know 1968

BLUE CAT
BS 103 Give It To Me 1968

PYRAMID
PYR 6062 Easy Come Easy Go 1968

CALTONE
TONE 119 I Love No Other Girl 1968

BLUE CAT
BS 100 Shake It Up 1968
BS 105 Whip Them 1968

AMALGAMATED
AMG 811 Give Me A Little Loving 1968
AMG 835 Mama Look Deh 1969
AMG 840 Who The Cap Fit 1969
AMG 850 Alli Button 1969

TROJAN
TR-672 Long Shot Kick The Bucket 1969
TR-685 Black Bud 1969
TR-698 Poor Rameses 1969
TR-7710 Samfie Man 1970
TR-7739 Driven Back 1970
TR-7760 Battle Of The Giants 1970
TR-7795 I Need Your Sweet Inspiration 1970
TR-7825 Let Your Yeah Be Yeah 1971
TR-7846 Give And Take 1971

SUMMIT
SUM 8511 Starvation 1971

TROJAN
TR-7855 You Don't Know Like I Know 1972
TR-7860 Roll Muddy River 1972
TR-7880 I Believe In Love 1972

DISCOGRAPHY ALBUMS 1968-1972

AMALGAMATED
AMGLP-2003 Greetings From The Pioneers 1968

TROJAN
TBL-103 Long Shot 1969
TRLS-24 Yeah 1971
TRLS-48 I Believe 1972

JIMMY CLIFF

Jimmy Cliff (James Chambers) was born on the 1st April 1948 in the Somerton district of St James Jamaica. He began writing songs from an early age whilst still at primary school. Moving to the capital in 1962 he sought out producers whilst he was still at Kingston Technical School, always trying but without success to get his songs recorded.

He entered many talent contests but his first break came when he met Leslie Kong and they decided to get into the music business. It was his third single, the first two were unsuccessful that launched him onto the music scene in Jamaica with 'Hurricane Hattie' a single that became a huge hit for Jimmy in Jamaica at the tender age of 14.

The record was produced by the emerging Leslie Kong who Jimmy would continue to work with right up until Kong's untimely death from a heart attack in 1971. Other hits followed in Jamaica for Jimmy with 'King Of Kings', 'Dearest Beverley' and 'Miss Jamaica'.

His success led to a contract with Island records and a promising move to the UK, but his career did not blossom, as Island tried to promote him as a rock star for a time, that was until the release of his first album, 'Hard Road To Travel'. A single titled 'Waterfall' was then followed up in 1969 by his international hit single 'Wonderful World Beautiful People' released on Trojan TR-690 and gaining a respectable number 6 in the UK chart in November that year. Further singles followed including 'Vietnam' and a cover of Cat Stevens 'Wild World' released on Island WIP-6087, reaching number 8 in September 1970.

Singer songwriter Cliff penned numerous hits including Desmond Dekker's massive chart success 'You Can Get It If You Really Want', 'Wonderful World Beautiful People' and 'Many Rivers To Cross' both sung by Cliff himself and 'Give And Take' by The Pioneers.

Jimmy Cliff's first entry into the UK chart during October 1970, 'Wonderful World Beautiful People' spent a total of thirteen weeks on the chart. Other reggae to feature the week it peaked at number 6 on the 29th November were The Upsetters 'Return Of Django' and Harry J Allstars 'Liquidator' currently at number 46 but destined for the top ten.

The UK chart looked like this on the 22nd November 1969:

1. Archies - Sugar Sugar
2. The Tremeloes - (Call Me) Number One
3. Fleetwood Mac - Oh Well
4. The Beatles - Something/Come Together
5. **Upsetters- Return Of Django / Dollar In The Teeth**
6. **Jimmy Cliff - Wonderful World Beautiful People**
7. Jethro Tull - Sweet Dream
8. Karen Young - Nobody's Child
9. Kenny Rogers / The First Edition - Ruby Don't Take Your Love To Town
10. Stevie Wonder - Yester-Me Yester-You Yesterday

'Vietnam' would become a second chart entry for Jimmy Cliff in February 1970 albeit only reaching number 46 and spending just three weeks on the chart.

Island records issued a cover version of a Cat Stevens song 'Wild World' a release that saw Jimmy Cliff back in the charts with the record peaking at number 8 in September 1970 and spending a total of thirteen weeks on the chart. Several excellent singles followed over the next couple of years, most notable of these were 'Struggling Man' released on Island, but further chart success eluded him.

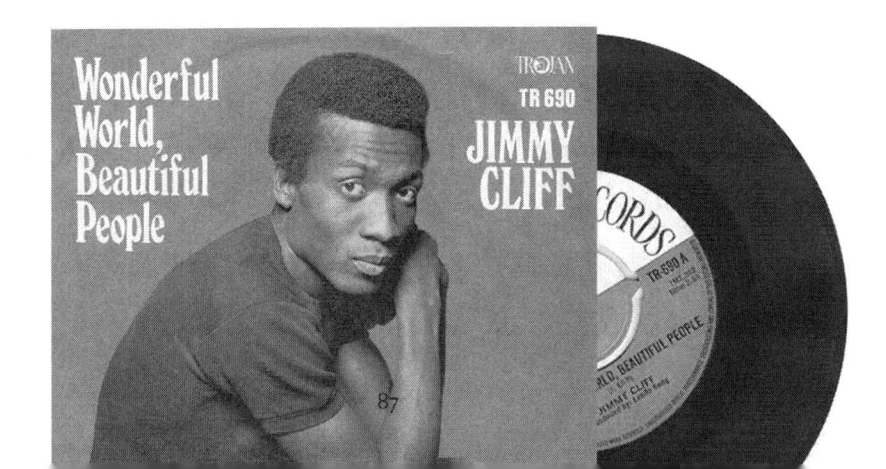

The British chart of the 12th September 1970 looked like this:

1. Smokey Robinson And The Miracles - Tears Of A Clown
2. Elvis Presley - The Wonder Of You
3. Three Dog Night - Mama Told Me (Not To Come)
4. Chairman Of The Board - Give Me Just A Little More Time
5. Bread - Make It With You
6. Freda Payne - Band Of Gold
7. Chicago - 25 Or 6 To 4
8. **Jimmy Cliff - Wild World**
9. Marmalade - Rainbow
10. Hot Chocolate - Love Is Life

1972 saw Jimmy Cliff become a truly international star as he played Ivanhoe 'Ivan' Martin in the film 'The Harder They Come'. Directed by the late Perry Henzell the film tells the story of a young man drawn to the ghettos of Kingston from the country by the promise of making it in the record business. Success does not come and he inevitably turns to a life of crime. The soundtrack elevated reggae to the world stage and still remains one of the most significant works to have come out of Jamaica.

Jimmy ended his association with Island Records after the filming of 'The Harder They Come' as he was near broke and asked Chris Blackwell for £50,000 to remain with Island. Chris Blackwell told him that he would soon make that sort of money but Jimmy could not wait and left the label. Within a few days of Jimmy leaving the label Island had found a new star in the making.

Having released several singles on Trojan and Pama's subsidiary labels Bob Marley found himself stranded in the UK whilst on tour. The story goes that he walked into Blackwell's office and left with £4,000 to record an album back in Jamaica, and the rest they say is history.

SINGLES DISCOGRAPHY 1968 -1972

ISLAND
WIP-6039 Waterfall 1968
WIP-6024 That's The Way Life Goes 1968

TROJAN
TR-690 Wonderful World Beautiful People 1969
TR-7767 You Can Get It If You Really Want 1969

ISLAND
WIP-6087 Wild World 1970

TROJAN
TR-7722 Vietnam 1970
TR-7745 Sufferin' In The Land 1970
TR-7845 Those Good Good Old Days 1971

ISLAND
WIP-6097 Synthetic World 1971
WIP-6103 Goodbye Yesterday 1971
WIP-6110 Sitting In Limbo 1971
WIP-6132 Struggling Man 1972

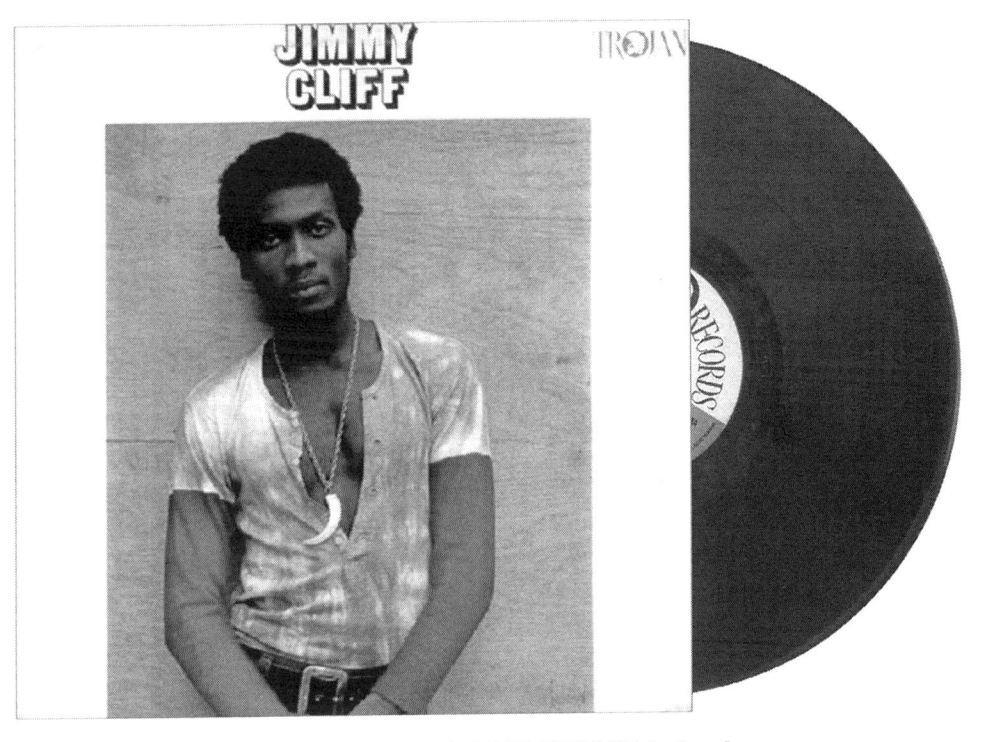

JIMMY CLIFF JIMMY CLIFF TROJAN RECORDS TRLS 16 1969

Side 1
1. TIME WILL TELL
2. MANY RIVERS TO CROSS
3. VIETNAM
4. USE WHAT I GOT
5. HARD ROAD TO TRAVEL

Side 2
1. WONDERFUL WORLD BEAUTIFUL PEOPLE
2. SUFFERIN' IN THE LAND
3. HELLO SUNSHINE
4. MY ANCESTORS
5. THAT'S THE WAY LIFE GOES
6. COME INTO MY LIFE

BOB AND MARCIA

'Young Gifted And Black' - with strings attached. Bob And Marcia's upbeat version of Nina Simone's black power song took the charts by storm and heralded the era of strings attached. The UK version with a vivacious rhythm complete with violins demonstrated the effects of the pop influence from Trojan on the true sound of Jamaica, a sound that can be summed up on the original Jamaican version of the single. One could argue that if it had not been such an upbeat sweetened version then it would probably have not gained chart success, therefore holding back further interest in reggae music from the mainstream. Importantly the sound was still popular with the all important skinheads.

The success was followed up with the duos second hit 'Pied Piper'. 'Young Gifted And Black' entered the charts on the 14th March 1970 reaching number 5 in April spending a total of twelve weeks on the chart. 'Pied Piper' followed in 1971 reaching number 11 in May, the duo's chart success covering a total of twenty three weeks during 1970 and 1971.

Other hits deserted them as reggae was by now beginning to evolve again with Trojan in particular developing a more sophisticated sound, a sound which did bring some initial success for groups such as Greyhound, The Pioneers and Dandy Livingstone but would ultimately disenchant reggae's loyal following of skinheads and the diehard West Indians who shared the love of the true sounds of Jamaica.

The pop influenced sound of the duos hits to the uninitiated of reggae from the early years gave a perception that they were just a flash in the pan, however nothing could be further removed from reality. Marcia Griffiths had begun her singing career having been born in Kingston Jamaica into what was described as a house full of music and love.

Her singing began in the church choir where her talent was quickly spotted. She soon signed with Coxsone Dodd's Studio One. Her first success came in 1968 with 'Feel like Jumping'. Further records rapidly followed with 'Truly', 'Tell Me Now' and a duet with Bob Andy 'Always Together'. A move to Harry Johnson 'Harry J' came in 1969 and after a couple of solos she recorded 'Young Gifted And Black' with Bob Andy, the track later released on Trojan with the strings added in the UK by Johnny Arthey. The duo toured the UK and signed a contract with CBS, a move that was to hinder more success and the partnership came to an end. Marcia went on to enjoy great achievements with a solo career and also became a member of Bob Marley's I Threes.

Bob Andy began his career as one of the original members of The Paragons a group which included John Holt and had a whole string of Jamaican hits during the early sixties, including 'The Tide Is High'. Bob decided to pursue a solo career and joined Coxone Dodd's Studio One where he remained until 1968, producing for Rupie Edwards.

The top ten week commencing the 4th April 1970 saw 'Young Gifted And Black' peak at number 5 amongst stiff competition from some old heavyweights, whilst Boris Gardner featured in the charts, currently at number 28 with his skinhead favourite, 'Elizabethan Reggae'.

1. Simon And Garfunkle – Bridge Over Troubled Waters
2. Mary Hopkin – Knock Knock Who's There
3. Andy Williams – Can't Help Falling In Love
4. Lee Marvin – Wand'rin' Star
5. **Bob And Marcia – Young Gifted And Black**
6. Pickettywitch – The Same Old feeling
7. The Beatles – Let It Be
8. Kenny Rogers And The First Edition – Something's Burning
9. The Dave Clark Five – Everybody Get Together
10. Elvis Presley – Don't Cry Daddy

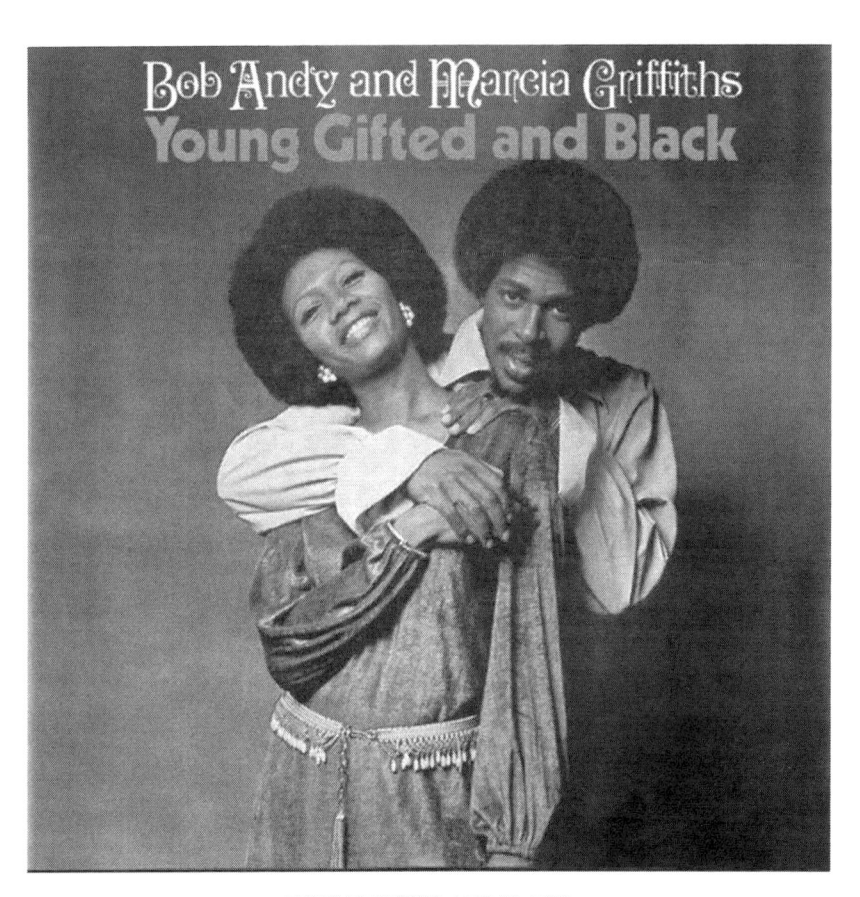

YOUNG GIFTED AND BLACK
TROJAN RECORDS TBL 122
Released 1970

SINGLES DISCOGRAPHY 1968-1972

MARCIA GRIFFITHS

COXONE
CS-7035 Mojo Girl 1968

BAMBOO
BAM-59 Shimmering Star 1970

HARRY J
HJ-6613 Put A Little Love In Your Heart 1970
HJ-6623 Band Of Gold 1970

BOB ANDY

DOCTOR BIRD
DB-1191 Games People Play 1969

BOB AND MARCIA

BAMBOO
BAM-40 Always Together 1970

HARRY J
HJ-6605 Young Gifted And Black 1970
HJ-6615 Got To Get Ourselves Together 1970

TROJAN
TR-7818 Pied Piper 1971
TR-7854 But I Do 1972

NICKY THOMAS

Nicky Thomas was born Cecil Nicholas Thomas in Portland Jamaica in 1949. Like some of his future compatriots of the reggae era Nicky had began his working life as a labourer where he would form an acquaintance with members of the future group The Gladiators.

His first recording to be a hit at home in Jamaica 'Run Nigel Run' was produced by Derrick Harriott, before starting out with his long association with Joe Gibbs, a union which was to provide Nicky with his most successful recording, 'Love Of The Common People'. Joe Gibbs was a seasoned record producer in Jamaica but 'Love Of The Common People' was his first taste of success in the UK. The UK Trojan release of the record was very pop infused, a version of the Jamaican release with strings added, a successful technique that was used on other singles that made the top thirty. The record allowed Nicky's very distinctive soul-full voice to shine through selling over 175,000 copies and made him an overnight sensation.

A tour of the UK followed prompting him to remain in England where he would continue to release other singles and albums. Surprisingly future chart success eluded him despite a string of excellent releases including 'If I Had A Hammer' and 'Yesterday Man', a record that flirted for a while but just failed to make the charts. Trojan subsequently released the album TBL 143 'Love of The Common People' in 1970 produced by Joe Gibbs. By 1971 Nicky was producing for himself and released a single 'Tell It Like It Is / BBC', a record incidentally that was directing harsh criticism at the BBC for the lack of airplay for reggae. A new album titled 'Tell It Like It Is' was released in 1972 featuring tracks that were self produced.

Many of Trojan's compilation albums featured Nicky's work, including the very popular 'Reggae Chartbusters' series. As a consequence of his untimely death in 1990 the world of reggae lost one its famous sons, a very talented performer who had helped elevate reggae to the mainstream in the early 1970s.

The British charts looked like this on the 11th July 1970:

1. Mungo Jerry - In The Summertime
2. Free - All Right Now
3. Mr Bloe - Groovin With Mr Bloe
4. Creedence Clearwater Revival - Up Around The Bend
5. The Four Tops - It's All In The Game
6. The Beach Boys - Cottonfields
7. Gerry Monroe - Sally
8. Cliff Richard – Goodbye Sam Hello Samantha
9. **Nicky Thomas – Love Of The Common People**
10. Fleetwood Mac – The Green Manalishi

SINGLES DISCOGRAPHY 1970-1972

TROJAN

TR-7750 Love Of The Common People   1970
TR-7796 God Bless The Children   1970
TR-7807 If I Had A Hammer   1970
TR-7830 Tell It Like It Is   1971
TR-7850 Yesterday Man   1971
TR-7878 Images Of You   1972

LOVE OF THE COMMON PEOPLE   NICKY THOMAS
TROJAN RECORDS TBL 143   Released 1970

Side 1
1. GOD BLESS THE CHILDREN
2. RAINY NIGHT IN GEORGIA
3. IF I HAD A HAMMER
4. TURN BACK THE HANDS OF TIME
5. DOING THE MOON WALK
6. LOVE OF THE COMMON PEOPLE

Side 2
1. MAMA'S SONG
2. HAVE A LITTLE FAITH
3. DON'T TOUCH
4. LONELY FEELIN'
5. I WHO HAVE NOTHING
6. LET IT BE
7. RED EYE

THE HISTORY OF SKINHEAD REGGAE 1968-1972   NICKY THOMAS

TELL IT LIKE IT IS   NICKY THOMAS
TROJAN RECORDS TRLS 25
Released 1972

THE HISTORY OF SKINHEAD REGGAE 1968-1972   NICKY THOMAS

Side 1
1. TELL IT LIKE IT IS   2. WATCH THAT LITTLE GIRL
3. DEEP IN THE MORNING   4. YESTERDAY MAN   5. WE PEOPLE
6. LAY LADY LAY IN THE MIDNIGHT HOUR (MEDLEY)

Side 2
1. JUST BECAUSE YOUR LOVE HAS GONE   2. SOUL POWER
3. I CAN'T STAND IT   4. ISN'T IT A PITY   5. BBC
6. LOVE PEACE AND HAPPINESS

DAVE AND ANSEL COLLINS

Dave Barker, born David Crooks in 1948 was raised by his grandmother from the age of 4 after his parents had emigrated. He soon discovered a talent for singing as a teenager with his musical career unfolding when he formed a group known as The Two Tones, although recording success eluded them.

He then spent some time with Winston Riley's Techniques, forming a duo with Glen Brown. It was whilst working in the pressing plant at Studio One that he was introduced to Lee 'Scratch' Perry, eventually becoming a regular vocalist. Perry suggested he change his name and record as Dave Barker. He was given every encouragement to develop a style of deejay vocals with the ensuing hit single 'Shocks Of A Mighty' a track that would later feature on Tighten Up Volume 3.

Ansel Collins, sometimes spelt Ansell or Ansil was also born in Kingston Jamaica in 1949. He began performing with The Invincibles then after a spell working with Lee 'Scratch' Perry he teamed up with Dave Barker where his keyboard playing epitomized the new style of skinhead reggae.

The famous reggae double act was often assumed to be brothers. They joined forces in 1971 to release 'Double Barrel' a track that was penned way back in 1968 but never released. 'Double Barrel' catapulted the duo to the world stage reaching number 22 on the Billboard charts in America, and reaching number 1 in Jamaica.

Perhaps more importantly to the skinheads and a wider audience 'Double Barrel' entered the British charts where it would spend two weeks at the top of the pile during May 1971. The record gained the distinction of being the first reggae record to chart on both sides of the Atlantic at the same time.

The follow up release also brought further chart success in the UK and international recognition with 'Monkey Spanner' a record in a similar style reaching a respectful number 7 in July the same year.

The duo were in Jamaica when the news hit that Double Barrel had taken off and were hurriedly flown to England by Winston Riley, that was once a passport could be sorted for Dave Barker. As soon as the Boeing landed they were whisked off to the Top of The Pops BBC studio to mime for the cameras, their first taste of a chilly England. They spent several weeks touring for Trojan before returning briefly to Jamaica recording tracks for their forthcoming album, not surprisingly titled 'Double Barrel' although ironically the LP ultimately consisted of previously recorded material written by Winston Riley.

After the release of the album and a handful of singles the pair parted company with Collins returning to Jamaica to become a session player.

The pinnacle of chart success for Trojan and reggae came in May 1971 when 'Double Barrel' peaked and spent two weeks at number 1. The chart also featured Bruce Ruffin's 'Rain' making a brief incursion at number 42.

The chart on May 1st 1971 looked like this:

1. **Dave And Ansel Collins - Double Barrel**
2. T Rex - Hot love
3. Dawn - Knock Three Times
4. The Rolling Stones - Brown Sugar/ Bitch / Let It Rock
5. Waldo de Los Rios - Mozart Symphony No 40
6. Ray Stevens - Bridget The Midget
7. Ringo Starr - It Don't Come Easy
8. Andy Williams – (Where Do I Begin) Love Story
9. Diane Ross – Remember Me
10. CCS – Walkin'

Monkey Spanner came hot on the heels of Double Barrel entering the charts on the 20th June 1971, eventually reaching number 7 on the 17th July where it stayed for three weeks, spending, a total of twelve weeks on the charts, ten of those in the top 30.

1. Middle Of The Road – Chirpy Chirpy Cheep Cheep
2. The Sweet – Co-Co
3. Hurricane Smith – Don't Let It Die
4. T Rex – Get It On
5. Lobo – Me And You And A Dog Named Boo
6. **Greyhound – Black And White**
7. **Dave And Ansel Collins – Monkey Spanner**
8. Blue Mink – Banner Man
9. John Kongos – He's Gonna Step On You Again
10. Tami Lynn – I'm Gonna Run Away From You

DISCOGRAPHY SINGLES 1968 -1972

DAVE BARKER
PUNCH
PH-20 Prisoner Of Love 1969

ACKEE
ACK-113 Johnny Dollar 1970
ACK-119 Life Of A Millionaire 1970

HIGH NOTE
HI-049 She Want It 1970

JACKPOT
JP-736 The Fastest Man Alive 1970
JP-742 Wet Version 1970
JP-745 Girl Of My Dreams 1970

PUNCH
PH-42 Reggae Meeting 1970

UPSETTER
US-331 Shocks Of A Mighty (UPSETTERS) 1970
US-358 Shocks 71 1971

SUPRREME
SUP-228 Double Heavy 1971

JACKPOT
JP-803 You'll Be Sorry 1972

ANSEL COLLINS
J-DAN
JDN-4401 Cock Robin 1970

TECHNIQUES
TE-913 Nuclear Weapon 1971

DAVE AND ANSEL COLLINS
TECHNIQUES
TE-901 Double Barrel 1971
TE-914 Monkey Spanner 1971
TE-915 Karate 1971

DOUBLE BARREL DAVE AND ANSEL COLLINS
TROJAN RECORDS TBL 162
(Issued on the TECHNIQUES label) Released 1971

Side 1
1. DOUBLE BARREL 2. WILD BUNCH 3. ELFREGO BACCA
4. MONKEY SPANNER VERSION 5. MY BEST GIRL
6. SECRET WEAPON

Side 2
1. I THE THIRD 2. THAT GIRL 3. IMPOSSIBLE MISSION
4. TEN TO ONE 5. I CAN COUNT THE DAYS 6 TWO FOUR ONE

GREYHOUND

Greyhound launched their musical life as 'The Rudies' in the late 60s, a group formed by Freddie Notes and British based musicians, Earl Dunn, Trevor Ardley White and Sonny Binns.

They were to enjoy several record releases but by far their most successful was a cover version of Bobby Bloom's 'Montego Bay' a record that achieved a top ten hit for Bobby Bloom in 1970 reaching number 3 in October that year, spending nineteen weeks in the charts. However Freddie Notes and the Rudies cover version released on Trojan TR-7791 achieved only a modest chart entry reaching number 45, charting for only two weeks in the same month, a month incidentally that saw Desmond Dekker and Horace Faith riding high.

Further singles followed including 'Patches' issued on Trojan TR-7798 which featured on 'Reggae Chartbusters Volume 2' but further chart success eluded them. Freddie Notes And The Rudies had an album released on Trojan in 1970 'Unity' TBL 107.

1971 witnessed a parting of the ways for The Rudies, Freddie Notes had left with Glenroy Oakley replacing him so they felt a change of identity was needed, a change that was to launch a reggae group who would have a relatively successful period over the next couple of years. The name was of course Greyhound.

The first success for Greyhound came with a cover version of a song written in 1955 titled 'Black And White', a record the group felt suited perfectly a pop-reggae style and sure enough it proved to be a massive hit for Greyhound. The track was released on Trojan TR-7820 on both the 'orange and white' label and the 'brown' label. The record entered the charts in June 1971 achieving a respectable two weeks at number 6 during July, spending a total of thirteen weeks on the chart.

The story behind 'Black And White' stemmed from America where in 1954 The Supreme Court outlawed segregation of public schools. It was originally published as a song in 1956, penned by David Arkin with Earl Robinson's music.

Their next success would come with another reggae version of a well known song, and one that suited the pop-reggae idiom superbly, 'Moon River'. A cover of a Henry Mancini number this time released as a Trojan Maxi single TR-7848 C/W 'I've been Trying' and 'Keep The Pressure On'. It achieved a top 12 for Greyhound in February 1972 and everything seemed to be going well, including a new album release on Trojan, 'Black And White' TRL-27.

Greyhound were however to achieve only one more chart success and it followed on the heels of 'Moon River'. Just as 'Moon River' was dropping out of the charts 'I Am What I Am' entered peaking at number 20 in April 1972. Released on Trojan TR-7853 it was their last recording for the label and within a year the group had broken up.

FREDDIE NOTES AND THE RUDIES, MONTEGO BAY was released in 1970 on Trojan TR-7791

BLACK AND WHITE

The British charts looked good for reggae during July 1971 with two records in the top 10, Greyhound had peaked at number 6 and Monkey Spanner was riding high at number 7.

1. T Rex - Get It On
2. Middle Of The Road - Chirpy Chirpy Cheep Cheep
3. The Sweet - Co-Co
4. Lobo - Me And You And A Dog Named Boo
5. Hurricane Smith - Don't Let It Die
6. **Greyhound - Black And White**
7. **Dave And Ansel Collins - Monkey Spanner**
8. New World - Tom Tom Turnaround
9. Blue Mink - Banner Man
10. The Temptations - Just My Imagination

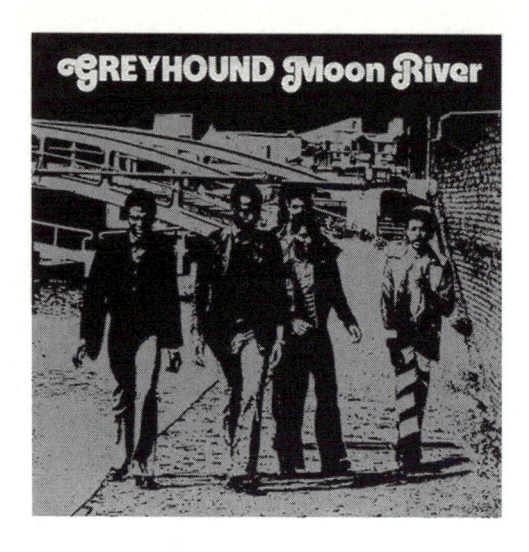

THE HISTORY OF SKINHEAD REGGAE 1968-1972   GREYHOUND

'Moon River' released as a Trojan Maxi single TR-7848 in 1971 with the B side featured two tracks, 'I've Been Trying' and 'Keep The Pressure On' peaked at number 12 on both the 5th and 19th of February, spending a total of eleven weeks on the charts. 'Moon River' was the second of a hat-trick of hits for Greyhound. The single released on the traditional TR label as well as the colourful Trojan Maxi label also came with an additional picture sleeve option available.

1. Chickory Tip - Son Of My Father
2. T Rex - Telegram Sam
3. The Chi-Lites - Have You Seen Her
4. Slade - Look Wot You Dun
5. Neil Reid - Mother Of Mine
6. Don McLean - American Pie
7. The New Seekers - I'd Like To Teach The World To Sing
8. Sonny And Cher - All I Ever Need Is You
9. Fortunes - Storm In A Teacup
10. Al Green - Let's Stay Together
11. America - Horse With No Name
12. **Greyhound - Moon River**

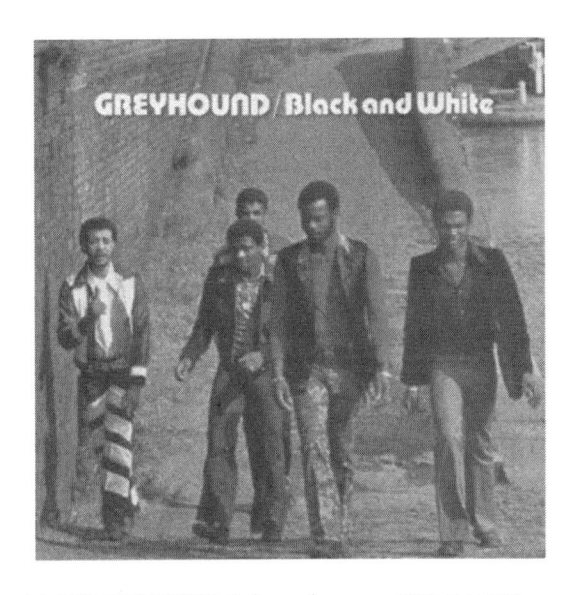

BLACK AND WHITE Released 1972 on TROJAN TRL 27

Side 1.
1. BLACK AND WHITE   2. LOVE IS BLUE   3. SAND IN YOUR SHOES
4. THE CHANGE   5. BE LOVING TO ME   6. YOU'RE THE ONE
Side 2
1. YESTERDAY'S LOVE   2. PEACE AND LOVE   3. MOON RIVER
4. FUNKY JAMAICA   5. HIGH AND DRY

'Moon River' was composed by Johnny Mercer (lyrics) and Henry Mancini (music) in 1961, the same year that Andy Williams first recorded the song.

DISCOGRAPHY SINGLES 1968-1972

FREDDIE NOTES AND THE RUDIES

GRAPE
GR-3010 Guns Of Navarone 1969

TROJAN
TR-7713 Shanghi 1969
TR-7734 Down On The Farm 1970
TR-7791 Montego Bay 1970
TR-7798 Patches 1970

GRAPE
GR-3011 Babylon 1970

'I Am What I Am' peaked at number 20 during April 1972 spending nine weeks on the chart. The chart of April 1972 also saw Johnny Nash 'Stir It Up' and Paul Simon's 'Mother And Child Reunion' feature.

GREYHOUND

TROJAN
TR-7820 Black And White 1971
TR-7848 Moon River 1971
TR-7853 I Am What I Am 1972

BLUE MOUNTAIN
BM-1016 Dream Lover 1972

TOOTS AND THE MAYTALS

Originally just called The Maytals their distinctive style of reggae combined with Frederick 'Toots' Hibbert's voice gave them a distinctive sound all of their own. Frederick grew up singing Gospel music with the church choir in the parish of Clarendon, Jamaica; he was one of seven children.

At the age of 16 he moved to Kingston where he meet Henry 'Raleigh' Gordon and Nathaniel 'Jerry' McCarthy, and the trio was born. Their first album 'Never Grow Old' was released in Jamaica during 1964 with great success. Their second album, produced by the legendry Byron Lee titled 'The Sensational Maytals', was released in 1965.

1966, yes that famous year in England was to see Frederick arrested and imprisoned for possession of marijuana in his native Jamaica, an incident that was to inspire one of his best loved tracks '54-46 That's My Number'.

Toots was arrested for possession of marijuana in 1966 but has always declared his innocence. "They frame me; they put something in my bag. It was a very cruel thin". The story goes that on the night he was arrested Hibbert says, he was on his way to a show and had stopped to bail a friend out of jail. He was carrying a bag containing his stage suit but neglected to bring his driver's licence. "The police told me I needed a licence to bail the person out, so I left my bag there and went back to get it. When I came back, they say they find ganja in it". It was while in prison that he penned the hit '54-46 That's My Number', the title of which was inspired by his prison identification number.

1967 saw him released from his custodial sentence with the band changing their name to Toots And The Maytals. Their next three albums were produced by Leslie Kong. In 1968 a record was released on the Pyramid label PYR-6057 that was claimed to have had a great influence on the name of the new beat that was replacing rocksteady, 'Do The Reggay'.

The first reggae record! When Toots was asked about 'Do The Reggay' being the first to evolve from rocksteady into reggae his response was, "People tell me that, but when I did it, I didn't know. There was the beat in Jamaica; reggae was played long before I started singing. And there was a slang, like a nickname for someone who don't dress properly - like if you are barefoot, people would call you 'streggae.' They say "hey, that guy is streggae, don't talk to him." If a girl don't dress properly, like don't have on any top, they call her streggae. So one morning, one Tuesday morning, we just said "Let's go along and do some reggae". Those days we'd just make stuff up, anything. A bird flies around the corner, you write a song about it. So we just say 'Do the reggay, do the reggay', and that's it. A few words, y'know? And nobody paid it any mind until it started to go all over the world. I saw it in the Guinness Book of Records. So I thank God that I did something good, and I didn't even plan it".

1970 saw the UK release of '54-46 That's My Number' originally released on the Pyramid label and featuring the rhythm track from Marcia Griffith's 'Feel Like Jumping' with a follow up single having a slight change of title and pace on Trojan TR-7808 '54-46 Was My Number' in late 1970. The lyrics to the record describing Toots time in prison and quoting his prison ID number was one of the first to achieve popularity outside of Jamaica.

Between the two '54-46' numbers they released 'Monkey Man', surprisingly The Maytals only British chart entry, the track also featured on Trojan's highly successful 'Reggae Chartbusters' Volume 2 in 1970. 'Monkey Man' reached number 47 in the UK Singles chart during that year, astonishingly only spending four weeks on the chart.

SWEET AND DANDY   BEVERLEY'S RECORDS   1969
Produced by Leslie Kong

Side 1
1. MONKEY MAN 2. PRESSURE DROP 3. I SHALL BE FREE
4. BLA BLA BLA 5. JUST TELL ME 6. WE SHALL OVERCOME

Side 2
1. SWEET AND DANDY 2. SCARE HIM 3. ALIDINA
4. I NEED YOUR LOVE 5. 54-46 THAT'S MY NUMBER
6. OH YEAH

MONKEY MAN TROJAN TBL 107 1970
Produced by Leslie Kong

Side 1
1. PEEPING TOM 2. REVIVAL REGGAE 3. GIVE PEACE A CHANCE
4. GOLD AND SILVER 5. THE PREACHER 6. BLA BLA BLA

Side 2
1. AFRICAN DOCTOR 2. MONKEY MAN 3. SUN MOON AND STAR
4. PRESSURE DROP 5. SHE'S MY SCORCHER
6. I SHALL BE FREE

DISCOGRAPHY SINGLES 1968-1972

PYRAMID
PYR-6043 Struggle 1968
PYR-6048 Just Tell Me 1968
PYR-6055 School Days 1968
PYR-6057 Do The Reggay 1968
PYR-6030 54-46 That's My Number 1968

NU BEAT
NB-031 My Testimony 1969

PYRAMID
PYR-6066 Don't Trouble Trouble 1969
PYR-6070 Alidina 1969
PYR-6073 Pressure Drop 1969
PYR-6074 Sweet And Dandy 1969

TROJAN
TR-7711 Monkey Man 1969
TR-7741 Bla Bla Bla 1970
TR-7786 Dr. Lester 1970
TR-7808 54-46 Was My Number 1970

SUMMIT
SUM-8510 Peeping Tom 1970
SUM-8527 It's You 1971

BLUE MOUNTAIN
BM-1020 Christmas Song 1972

HILLCREST
HCT-4 Hey Rasta Man 1972

SUMMIT
SUM-8533 Never You Change 1972
SUM-8537 It Must Be True love 1972

TROJAN
TR-7865 Louie Louie / Pressure Drop 72 1972

The Maytals had a cameo role in the 1972 film 'The Harder They Come' with both 'Sweet And Dandy' and 'Pressure Drop' featuring on the soundtrack.

The song, 'Sweet And Dandy' tells the story of a young couple about to get married, having last minute nerves. They couple are both pacified and encouraged on by their older relatives whilst all the while the guests are eager to celebrate the occasion. The conclusion sees the happy couple dancing.

JUDGE DREAD

Alexander Hughes was born on the 2nd May 1945 in Kent, although he will always be remembered as Judge Dread. Perhaps his biggest tribute was becoming the first white recording artist to have a hit in Jamaica with 'Big Six'. The Judge had several other accolades to his name including the greatest number of banned records by the BBC, running to a staggering total of eleven, coincidently the number of chart hits to his name.

He could also boast the greatest number of reggae records to enter the UK chart, no mean feat when you consider the competition from the likes of Desmond Dekker and Bob Marley to name just two.

During his teenage years he lodged with a West Indian family in Brixton and had his first introduction to Jamaican music. His early career was to some extent determined by his size, first a bouncer at a local club then spending time as a bodyguard for the likes of Prince Buster, Coxone Dodd and Duke Reid whilst they were touring Britain. Next up came a stint at wrestling, AKA The Masked Executioner, and a spell with Trojan as a debt collector.

A man of many talents he also had a session as a DJ on a local radio station and had his own sound system, but his 'BIG' break was about to come. Alex was infatuated by Prince Buster's ribald 'Big Five' so he went into the Trojan studio to record his own follow up using the rhythm track of Verne & Sons 'Little Boy Blue'.

The lyrics were a rude version of nursery rhymes and by out-and-out luck Trojan's Lee Gopthal came in during the recording.

The story goes that he was so impressed that he signed the DJ to the company, deciding to release 'Big Six'.

Alex chose to issue the record under his stage name of Judge Dread in honour of a character from Prince Buster. The record was released appropriately on Trojan's subsidiary Big Shot label BI-608.

THE HISTORY OF SKINHEAD REGGAE 1968-1972   JUDGE DREAD

The record sold well locally but a deal was then struck with EMI for distribution that would see the record take the charts by storm despite no air play as the BBC had banned the record. Trojan's devious attempts to convince otherwise that the record was not rude fell on the same deaf ears that had banned 'Wet Dream' some three years earlier.

The ban did not prevent the record becoming a hit, following as it did in the footsteps of Max Romeo's chart success of 1969, with 'Big Six' reaching number 11 in October 1972, spending some six months on the chart and selling a very creditable 300,000 copies.

For several years the sounds emanating from Jamaica were finding their way to these shores so it was somewhat of a coup that 'Big Six' became a huge hit in Jamaica, with Judge Dread finding himself in Kingston to perform before a live audience. No one had seen Judge Dread and it was reported that the crowd thought that the big guy roaming around on stage was in fact his bodyguard, until that was he grabbed the microphone and began.

The crowd were said to have been amazed as no one considered that the Judge could be white. The follow up in the UK also on Big Shot BI-613 was understandably titled 'Big Seven' following in the same vein this time using the rhythm from 'My Conversation' originally released in 1968 by the Uniques. 'Big Seven' did better despite its inevitable ban reaching number 18 in December 1972 before peaking at number 8 on the 13th January 1973.

The 'Judge' enjoyed further chart success over the coming years and continued touring, with his last appearance coming on the 13th March 1998 at The Penny Theatre in Canterbury. Judge Dread died of a heart attack as he was leaving the stage at the end of his performance, initially the audience thought it was part of his act, before they realised the seriousness of the situation.

CHARTBUSTERS - THE SINGLES THAT MADE THE TOP 30

The vinyl 45 or 7 inch was named after its play speed with the first 'single' produced in 1949 by RCA in America. The format soon took off with the young record buying public who preferred the smaller and cheaper 45 to the more expensive 12 inch LP. In Britain the sales of records increased providing competition for the USA but it was a tiny Island in the Caribbean that was witnessing a new revolution.

The sound system operators in Jamaica were turning their hand to record production, releasing an outpouring of ska, replacing the imported American R&B that had previously been the only source of music. The first recording studio to open in Jamaica was Ken Khouri 'Federal Records', recording mento music. 1954 saw Jamaica's first record label 'Federal Records' launched by Khouri with Coxone Dodd and Duke Reid following suit. The music produced was a fusion of Caribbean and rhythm and blues and led to the development of bluebeat. The bass evolved to a more prominent feature and ska was born the forerunner of rocksteady and reggae.

The singles that made the charts come next, kicking off with perhaps the most iconic reggae sound even, for the uninitiated.

ISRAELITES   DESMOND DEKKER AND THE ACES
Released on PYRAMID PYR 6058 1968
Highest chart position 1 19/04/1969

Desmond Dekker was already a superstar in his native Jamaica courtesy of his hit song 'Music Like Dirt' winning the 1968 Jamaican Festival. The festival was inaugurated in 1962 to showcase performing artists by the Minister of Community Development, Edward Seaga who would eventually go onto become Prime Minister.

Desmond found favour in Britain where the mods embraced his music. In 1968, he released 'Israelites.' The record remained largely overlooked for many months. Nevertheless the song did eventually catch on, entering the charts on the 22nd of March 1969 and within four weeks it was at the top of the pile, albeit for just one week, spending seven weeks in the top 10. Israelites also found success across the Atlantic becoming the first true reggae sound to chart in America.

IT MIEK   DESMOND DEKKER AND THE ACES
Released on PYRAMID PRY 6068   1969
Highest chart position   7   26/07/1969

'It Miek', appearing on some labels as 'It Mek' was released in June 1969 and entered the charts in July, issued as the follow to up 'Israelites' by Desmond Dekker and The Aces. The song was written by Desmond and produced by Leslie Kong. The Aces became Desmond's backing group back in Jamaica as early as 1965 but when international recognition arrived the two members, Wilson James and Easton Barrington Howard, refused to travel to England, leaving Desmond's future recording career as a solo artist.

'It Miek' was laid down in Jamaica with the brass section added in the UK. 'It Miek' charted for eleven weeks and sold globally over a million copies. The song it telling of Desmond's little sister with the title 'Mek' being Jamaican patois for let us do it or make up your mind with many references telling of the song titles meaning as that's the reason. The last track to be released featuring the Aces was 'Pickney Gal' a record that surprisingly only made number 46, charting for only three weeks in January 1970.

THE HISTORY OF SKINHEAD REGGAE 1968-1972   CHARTBUSTERS

8. VANITY FARE - EARLY IN THE MORNING
9. LOVE AFFAIR - BRING BACK THE GOODTIMES
10. MAX ROMEO - WET DREAM
11. ELVIS PRESLEY - IN THE GHETTO
12. MARVIN GAYE - TOO BUSY THINKING 'BOUT
13. ZAGER AND EVANS - IN THE YEAR 2525
14. DONOVAN AND JEFF BECK - GOO GO

WET DREAM   MAX ROMEO
Released on UNITY UN-503 1968
Highest chart position 10 16/08/1969

'Wet Dream' was an up-tempo number with a very strong melody, almost unique at the time and had already become a massive hit in Jamaica before being released in the UK in 1968. Early sales of the record were slow but when it started to take off it was banned by the BBC with their DJ's Tony Blackburn and Alan Freeman instructed to make reference to the record only as 'a record by Max Romeo'. It has been well documented that 'Wet Dream' sold over 250,000 copies and remained on the chart for almost six months. In an interview in 2007 when asked why he recorded it Max is reported to have suggested the devil made him do it.

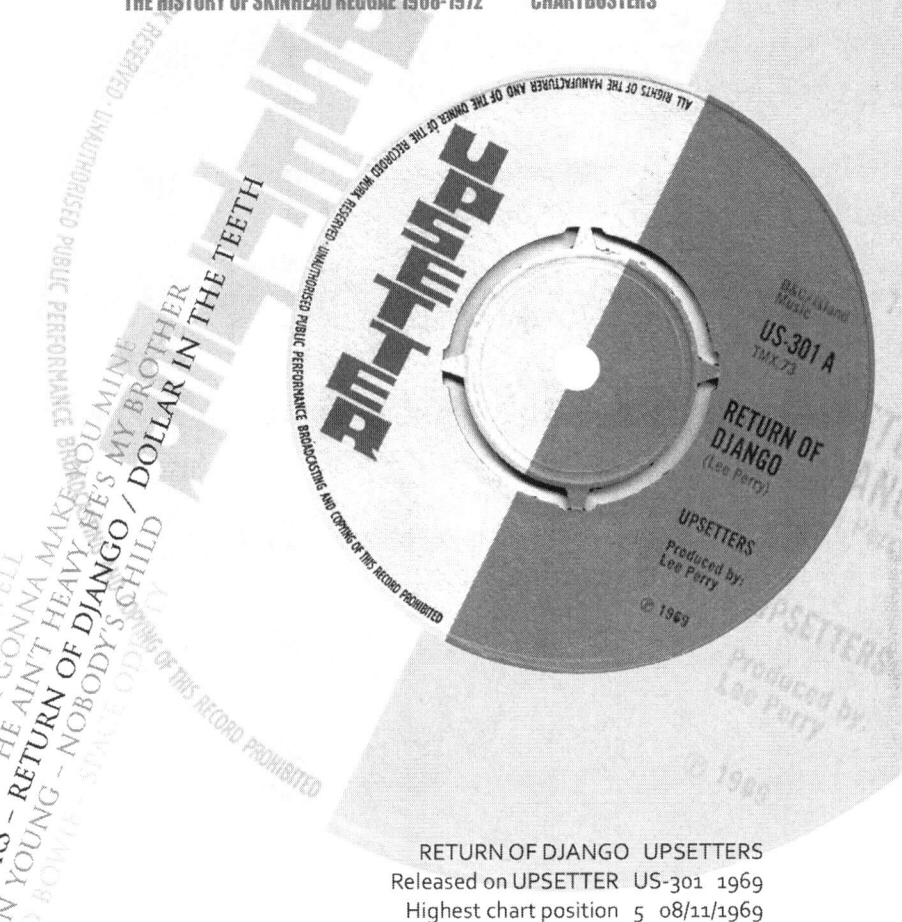

RETURN OF DJANGO UPSETTERS
Released on UPSETTER US-301 1969
Highest chart position 5 08/11/1969

The popularity of the music the skinheads had endeared themselves to was highlighted here when the instrumental 'Return Of Django' entered the charts on the 4th of October 1969, attaining the number 5 slot in November where it stayed for two weeks. 'Return Of Django' spent a total of fifteen weeks on the chart, no doubt assisted by the B side featuring 'Dollar In The Teeth'. The title track was a reference to the spaghetti western Django, released in 1966. The album of the same name was released by Trojan in 1970 on the Upsetter label TRLS 19.

LONG SHOT KICK THE BUCKET   THE PIONEERS
Released on TROJAN TR-672   1969
Highest chart position   21   15/11/1969

'Long Shot Kick The Bucket' a true classic skinhead reggae sound, was a sequel to the trios Jamaican hit 'Long Shot' released in 1968 on the Joe Gibbs Amalgamated label. The song related to the death of a horse at Jamaica's famous Caymanas Park race course in Kingston. An instant hit in Jamaica, the record was released in the UK by Trojan and appeared on both the orange and orange and white labels. It was picked up by the independent radio stations but blatantly ignored by the BBC who did eventually yield and added it to their playlist.

The record entered the chats in October 1969 reaching number 21 and featured in the charts for eleven weeks. The appearance in the chart prompted Sidney, Jackie and George to fly to London to promote the record. Trojan released 'Long Shot' an album produced by Lesley Kong that including the single in late 1969.

WONDERFUL WORLD BEAUTIFUL PEOPLE   JIMMY CLIFF
Released on TROJAN TR-690   1969
Highest chart position   6   22/11/1969

Jimmy Cliff was an established star in Jamaica in 1962 at the tender age of 14 and released 'Wonderful World Beautiful People' in the UK on Trojan in 1969 and of course went on to feature on Trojan's first 'Reggae Chartbuster' album released in 1970. The song, very though provoking takes a look at the state of the world, and with an excellent beat, entered the charts in October 1969 where it would remain for thirteen weeks. Jimmy's next recording, his own penned song, 'You Can Get It If You Really Want' issued on Trojan never made the chart, although Desmond Dekker's version also released by Trojan a month later went on to become a massive international hit.

Jimmy's next release 'Vietnam', a protest song, sold well in America but only made the top 50 in the UK for three weeks during spring 1970, peaking at number 46. The track featured on Trojan's 1970 album, 'Reggae Chartbusters Volume 2'.

LIQUIDATOR HARRY J ALL STARS
Released on HARRY J TR-675 1969
Highest chart position 17 29/11/1969

Harry J Allstars included bassist 'Family Man' Aston Barrett, drummer Carlton Barrett and guitarist Alva Lewis who were originally the Hippy Boys. Aston 'Family Man' and his brother Carlton went on to form the core of The Wailers. The original version of the rhythm was taken from 'What Am I To Do' by Tony Scott. Harry Johnson acquired the rights to the tune and released it as The Harry J Allstars.

The tune found instant popularity with the skinheads and was adopted as an anthem at several football grounds throughout England during the early 70s. Accusations that the record fuelled violence amongst rival gangs eventually lead to its ban at many grounds. The Staple singers used the introduction and bass line for their 1972 hit, 'I'll Take You There'. 'Liquidator' entered the charts during October 1969 soon reaching number 9 in November and featured in the chart for a very respectable twenty weeks, finally dropping out in March 1970.

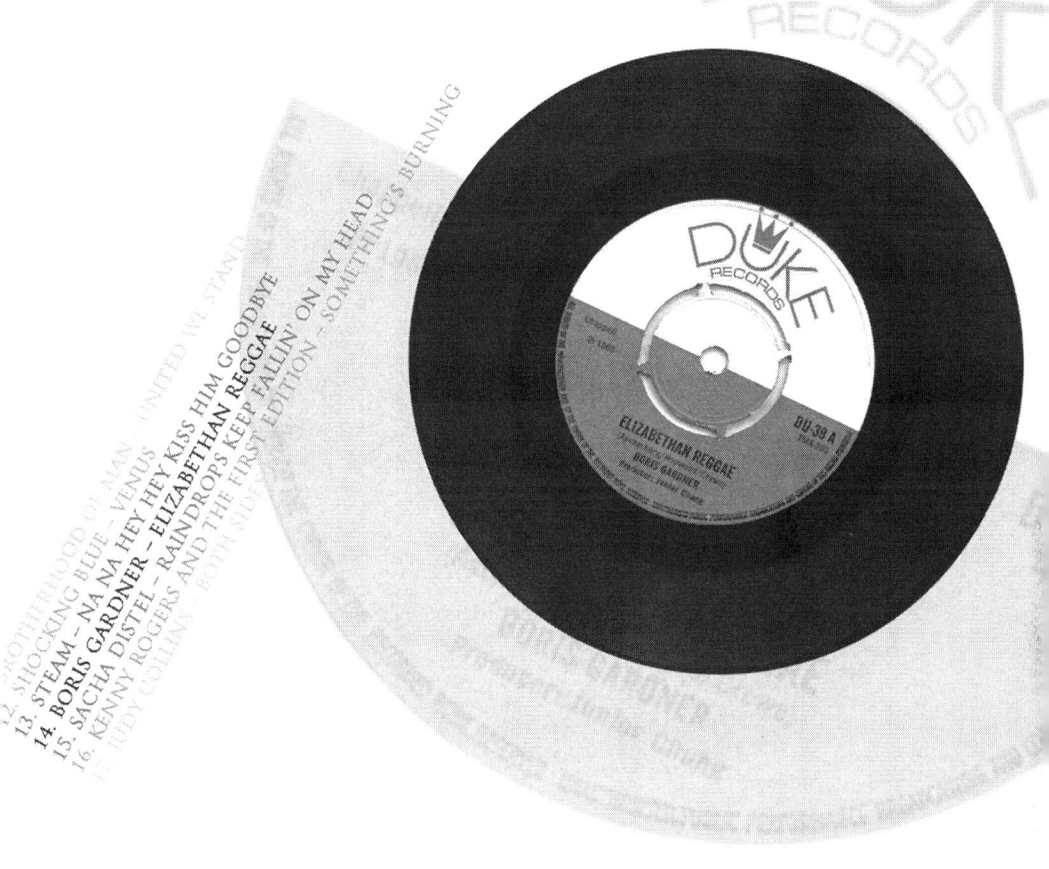

ELIZABETHAN REGGAE   BORIS GARDNER
Released on DUKE   DU-39   1969
Highest chart position   14   07/03/1970

The reggae version of the English composer Ronald Binge's 'Elizabethan Serenade' written in 1951 was released on the Duke label DU-39 in 1969. It immediately became a popular instrumental with the skinheads, and soon gained international recognition. The providence to the record though is in some doubt as the first pressings credited production of 'Elizabethan Reggae' to Byron Lee and the artist as being Byron Lee & The Dragonaires (spelt Dragonairs on the label) with the track appearing on the B side of DU-39. The A side featured 'Soul Serenade' by Byron Lee &The. Dragonaires

The record entered the chart at number 48 on the 17th January 1970 but dropped out only to re-enter on the 31st of January where it would remain roller coasting for the next twelve weeks, peaking at number 14. The chart from the 28th of February onward attributed 'Elizabethan Reggae' to Boris Gardner with production of the record credited to Junior Chung, the pressing now having 'Elizabethan Reggae' on the A side, and 'Soul Serenade' by Byron Lee & The Dragonaires on the B side, nevertheless still under the prefix DU-39.

THE HISTORY OF SKINHEAD REGGAE 1968-1972   CHARTBUSTERS

1. SIMON AND GARFUNKLE – KNOCK KNOC...
2. MARY HOPKIN – KNOCK KNOC...
3. ANDY WILLIAMS – CAN'T HELP FA...
4. LEE MARVIN – WAND'RIN' STAR
5. **BOB AND MARCIA – YOUNG GIFTED AN...**
6. PICKETTYWITCH – THE SAME OLD FEELING
7. THE BEATLES – LET IT BE
8. KENNY ROGERS AND THE FIRST EDITION – SOM...
9. THE DAVE CLARK FIVE – EVERYBODY GET TOGETHER
10. ELVIS PRESLEY – DON'T CRY DADDY

YOUNG GIFTED AND BLACK   BOB AND MARCIA
Released on HARRY J   HJ-6605   1970
Highest chart position   5   04/04/1970

'Young Gifted And Black' was a UK release of a Jamaican single with strings attached, and an upbeat version of Nina Simone's black power song. The stings were added in the UK for the release on Trojan's Harry J label. The original Jamaican version was sweetened for the general UK record buying public, the violins enhancing the vivacious rhythm. The record was a popular choice with the skinheads but a change in direction from the raw sounds of reggae. However had it been the genuine Jamaican article it may not have found favour outside the skinheads collection. The record entered the charts in March 1970 peaking at number 5 before falling back out in May.

LOVE OF THE COMMON PEOPLE   NICKY THOMAS
Released on TROJAN TR-7750 1970
Highest chart position 9 11/07/1970

Nicky Thomas will always be remembered for this wonderful adaptation of 'Love Of The Common People' a true reggae infused pop sound reaching number 9 in the UK and spending fourteen weeks on the chart during the summer of 1970. The song was originally penned by John Hurley and Ronnie Wilkins with The Everley Brothers releasing it as a single in 1967. The song tells of poverty and unemployment for USA families with mention of the USA governments free food tickets. It goes onto describe how their clothes were less than new and the lyrics were interpreted by many as a protest to life for the poor in the USA at that time. It would be the only chart success for Nicky although he would produce and release many excellent recordings including 'BBC', a record taking a swipe at the lack of air play for reggae on the nations number one station. The world of reggae lost one of its famous sons due to his untimely death in 1990.

THE HISTORY OF SKINHEAD REGGAE 1968-1972   CHARTBUSTERS

WILD WORLD   JIMMY CLIFF
Released on ISLAND   WIP-6087
Highest chart position   8   12/09/1970

A reunion with Island records in 1970 saw Jimmy Cliff's rendering of the Cat Stevens penned 'Wild World' released, some three months before Stevens' own version was released in America. Ironically Cat Stevens original single was never released in the UK at that time, the song featuring only as a track on an Island album. Jimmy Cliff's version remained on the chart for twelve weeks. 'Wild World' has been covered many times most notably by Maxi Priest who enjoyed success with his reggae hit in the 80s.

YOU CAN GET IT IF YOU REALLY WANT   DESMOND DEKKER
Released on TROJAN TR-7777 1970
Highest chart position 2 10/10/1970

The well documented 'You Can Get It If You Really Want' was Desmond's follow up to 'Pickney Gal' but this time without the backing of The Aces. Desmond had now moved to the UK following his previous recording success and the song penned by Jimmy Cliff would give him a number 2 hit, only eclipsed by Freda Payne's 'Band Of Gold'.

The story goes however that Desmond did not want to record the song; a complete change of direction from his earlier success' but was eventually persuaded to do so by his mentor and producer Leslie Kong. The same rhythm track is used for the record as was issued only a month earlier sung by Cliff himself for the song of the same title. TR-7777 entered the charts in August 1970 where it remained for fifteen weeks reaching number 2 for two weeks during October. An album of the same title followed, released on Trojan TBL 146 in November 1970. Jimmy Cliff's original version found fame featuring in the 1972 film 'The Harder They Come'.

THE HISTORY OF SKINHEAD REGGAE 1968-1972   CHARTBUSTERS

10. THE TEMPTATIONS – BALL OF C...
11. MATTHEW'S SOUTHERN COMFORT –
12. THE FAMILY – STRANGE BAND
13. **HORACE FAITH – BLACK PEARL**
14. CLARENCE CARTER – THE TIP OF MY FINGERS
15. DES O'CONNOR –
16. SMOKEY ROBINSON AND THE MIRACLES – TEARS OF A CLOWN

BLACK PEARL   HORACE FAITH
Released on TROJAN TR-7790   1970
Highest chart position   13   17/10/1970

This Johnny Arthey strings added version of a record by Sonny Charles & The Checkmates made it to number 13 in the UK on the 17th October 1970. The record was to some extent over cooked, and a far cry for the pure reggae that endeared the skinheads amongst others, but it did sell well and gained the only hit for Horace. It was described at the time as 'swamped with pop hooks' nevertheless it was a huge hit spending some ten weeks on the chart. 'Black Pearl' featured on 'Reggae Chartbusters Volume 2'.

DOUBLE BARREL DAVE AND ANSIL COLLINS
Released on TECHNIQUES TE-901 1971
Highest chart position 1 01/05/1971

Produced by Winston Riley and released both in Jamaica and the UK in 1970 'Double Barrel's' distinctive beat and Dave Barkers bellowing vocals were a recipe for success with the skinheads, declaring that he was the magnificent! The UK release was issued on Trojan's, Winston Riley's Techniques label and soon became an instant hit, with both Collins & Barker whisked off to Britain, once passports were sorted, with the duo taking the top spot on Top of The Pops. Although the new release seemed ahead of its time the track had been laid down some three years earlier in Jamaica, with Riley bringing in Barker to overdub the rhythm track.

The record featured Dave Barker vocals, Ansil Collins keyboard, and a 15-year-old Lowell 'Sly' Dunbar. A tour of the UK followed but the duo has always maintained that although the song was big they didn't get a great reward it monetary terms, now where has that been said before!

RAIN BRUCE RUFFIN
Released on TROJAN TR-7814   1971
Highest chart position 19 29/05/1971

'Rain' was released on Trojan TR-7814 with the B side featuring 'Geronimo'. The record enjoyed mediocre chart success featuring for eleven weeks in the early summer of 1971, its top spot being a respectable number 19. The song was a reggae cover of Jose' Feliciano's 1969 American hit.

Bruce moved to London following the chart success of 'Rain'. The track featured on the 1971 Trojan album 'Reggae Chartbusters Volume 3'.

PIED PIPER BOB AND MARCIA
Released on TROJAN TR-7818 1971
Highest chart position 11 10/07/1971

The second follow up to 'Young Gifted And Black' marked a return to chart success for the duo of Bob Andy and Marcia Griffiths. 'Pied Piper' continued the pop-reggae idiom, the up-tempo number following in a similar vein to the previous success entering the charts on the 5th of June 1971. It charted for thirteen weeks, peaking at number 11 in July.

'Pied Piper' was the last chart success for the duo who then signed with CBS, a move that did not work out well, and the pair parted musical company.

BLACK AND WHITE   GREYHOUND
Released on TROJAN TR-7820 1971
Highest chart position 6 17/07/1971

The first success for Greyhound came with a cover version of a song written in 1955 titled 'Black And White' a record the group felt suited perfectly a pop-reggae style and sure enough it proved to be a massive hit for Greyhound. Released on both the 'orange and white' Trojan label and the 'brown' label the record entered the charts in June 1971 achieving a respectable two weeks at number 6 during July, spending a total of thirteen weeks on the chart.

The story behind 'Black And White' stemmed from America where in 1954 The Supreme Court outlawed segregation of public schools. It was originally published as a song in 1956, penned by David Arkin with Earl Robinson's music.

MONKEY SPANNER   DAVE AND ANSEL COLLINS
Released on TECHNIQUES TE-914   1971
Highest chart position 7 17/07/1971

'Monkey Spanner' was the follow up to the massive number one hit 'Double Barrel' and would take the charts by storm, becoming a summer sensation and an anthem for the skinheads. 'Monkey Spanner', now credited to Ansel, entered the chart on the 26th of June 1971 where it remained for twelve weeks, its pinnacle of success at number 7 attained for three weeks during July. Like its predecessor 'Double Barrel', 'Monkey Spanner' featured an instrumental on the B side, 'Version 2'.

Chart success was not what the reggae sound was all about but by attaining the chart it presented a rare opportunity for its followers. They could hear reggae on national radio but perhaps more importantly see their idols on the television through the media of Top of The Pops, remember this was before video and decades before DVD became a part of everyday life.

THE HISTORY OF SKINHEAD REGGAE 1968-1972   CHARTBUSTERS

LET YOUR YEAH BE YEAH   THE PIONEERS
Released on TROJAN TR-7825 1971
Highest chart position 5 11/09/1971

'Let Your Yeah Be Yeah', a song penned by Jimmy Cliff
was the second of a hat-trick of hits for the Pioneers.
Featuring on the chart for twelve weeks it
rewarded the trio with appearances
on the BBC Top of The Pops.

140

THE HISTORY OF SKINHEAD REGGAE 1968-1972   CHARTBUSTERS

MOON RIVER GREYHOUND
Released on TROJAN MAXI TR-7848 1971
Highest chart position 12 05/02/1972

'Moon River' was the second of Greyhound's chart successes during the twilight years of skinhead reggae. The pop infused record was a hit for the group in early 1972. 'Moon River' enjoyed eleven weeks of charting reaching a respectable number 12, no mean feat given that the love affair was almost over with the reducing ranks of skinheads.

Released as a Trojan Maxi single the B side featured two tracks, 'I've Been Trying' and 'Keep The Pressure On'. As well as the colourful Trojan Maxi label an additional picture sleeve option was available.

MOTHER AND CHILD REUNION   PAUL SIMON
Released on CBS   CBS S 793   1972
Highest chart position   5   18/03/1972

Paul Simon travelled to Jamaica to cut a ska track 'Mother And Child Reunion' but when he arrived in the studio the musicians told him that ska was out, it's now reggae, so the song was recorded in reggae, apparently the first time Paul Simon had heard the term. Paul had wanted to get the authentic feel for the song using Jamaican musicians and recorded it at Dynamic studios in Kingston. It has been well documented that recording sessions would be held up when goats roamed through the studio and that the equipment was a far cry from what he was accustomed to in America, but it did manage to create an authentic track.

1. NILSSON - WITHOUT YOU
2. DON MACLEAN - AMERICAN PIE
3. THE NEW SEEKERS - BEG STEAL OR BORROW
4. CHICORY TIP - SON OF MY FATHER
5. PAUL SIMON - MOTHER AND CHILD REUNION
6. GILBERT O'SULLIVAN - HOME AGAIN (NATURALLY)
7. MICHAEL JACKSON - GOT TO BE THERE

The infectious upbeat sound of 'Mother And Child Reunion' was one of the very first reggae songs by a white American musician. Released in the UK on the CBS label it entered the charts on the 19th February 1972 peaking at number 5 four weeks later. It only spent twelve weeks on the chart but ten of those were it in the top 30. Trojan released their own up-tempo reggae version TR 7852 recorded by The Uniques, a group who had enjoyed considerable success during the rocksteady era. Although TR-7852 did not share the chart success of the original Paul Simon single it was a popular release finding its way onto 'Club Reggae Volume 3' and is included here as Sony Music Entertainment in America were unable grant permission to include the original label of the Paul Simon version.

STIR IT UP   JOHNNY NASH
Released on CBS   CBS S 7800   1972
Highest chart position   13   29/04/1972

'Stir It Up' was written by Bob Marley in 1967 and issued on Trojan TR-617 by The Wailers in 1968. It later featured on the legendary 'Catch A Fire' album released in 1973. CBS released 'Stir It Up' in the UK and it became a hit for Johnny Nash. The record spent twelve weeks on the chart but surprisingly only reached the moderate heights of number 13. Johnny Nash had enjoyed earlier chart success in the UK and America in 1968 with 'Hold Me Tight' reaching number 5 in the UK, a record that charted for sixteen weeks. 'You Got Soul' followed by 'Cupid' both gained the number 6 slot and coincidently both charted for twelve weeks in early 1969. Conceivably if 'Stir It Up' had been released earlier in the skinhead era it could well have topped the charts.

I AM WHAT I AM GREYHOUND
Released on TROJAN TR-7853 1972
Highest chart position 20 29/04/1972

Greyhound's third chart success would remain on the chart for nine weeks during the spring of 1972 but it only achieved a mediocre top 20 position. This was an indication of things to come for a year or so earlier this would surely have been a top ten hit, continuing in the pop-reggae idiom. It was to be one of the last before a complete change in style to what has already been described as 'string laden and watered down'. It was a direction that saw the remaining skinheads, who by now were some of a new generation of the traditional skinheads, some following on from their brothers, becoming disillusioned with the sound, some hanging onto the lasting hope for a resurgence of the original skinhead era which never came.

THE HISTORY OF SKINHEAD REGGAE 1968-1972 **CHARTBUSTERS**

MAD ABOUT YOU BRUCE RUFFIN
Released on RHINO RNO 101 1972
Highest chart position 9 29/07/1972

'Mad About You' featured for twelve weeks on the chart although this was pure pop reggae, a far cry from the reggae-pop infused sounds of Greyhound and the Pioneers. 'Mad About You' achieved the lofty heights of number 9 but it was a very 'polished-sweetened' reggae sound that the ebbing band of followers could no longer empathise with. Gone had the raw sounds and incessant rhythms, setting it apart from the mainstream.

6. ALICE COOPER – SCHOOL'S OUT
7. JOHNNY NASH – I CAN SEE CLEARLY NOW
8. THE NEW SEEKERS – CIRCLES
9. BRUCE RUFFIN – MAD ABOUT YOU
10. DAVID BOWIE – STAR MAN
11. THE SWEET – LITTLE WILLY
12. HAWKWIND – SILVER MACHINE

THE HISTORY OF SKINHEAD REGGAE 1968-1972   CHARTBUSTERS

2. GARY GLITTER – ROCK AND ROLL PARTS 1 AND 2
3. DR HOOK AND THE MEDICINE SHOW – SYLVIA'S MOTHER
4. THE NEW SEEKERS – CIRCLES
5. JOHNNY NASH – I CAN SEE CLEARLY NOW
6. THE SWEET – LITTLE WILLY

I CAN SEE CLEARLY NOW   JOHNNY NASH
Released on CBS   CBS S 8113   1972
Highest chart position   5   29/07/1972

Johnny Nash was back in the charts again in June 1972 with his own penned song 'I Can See Clearly Now' taken from his album of the same name, recorded in London the same year. The record featured on the charts for fifteen weeks reaching the lofty height of number 5.

146

THE HISTORY OF SKINHEAD REGGAE 1968-1972   CHARTBUSTERS

SUZANNE BEWARE OF THE DEVIL   DANDY LIVINGSTONE
Released on HORSE   HOSS 16   1972
Highest chart position   14   07/10/1972

No stranger to the reggae scene but surprisingly it had taken the entire era of skinhead reggae before producer and singer Dandy Livingstone, AKA Dandy enjoyed top thirty chart success. It was achieved with 'Suzanne Beware Of The Devil' a record issued on Trojan's charismatic Horse label that first charted in September 1972 where it remained for eleven weeks. Much of Dandy's work featured on Trojan's compilation albums.

BIG SIX   JUDGE DREAD
Released on BIG SHOT   BI-608   1972
Highest chart position   11   14/10/1972

Alex Hughes was infatuated by Prince Buster's ribald 'Big Five' and recorded his own follow up using the rhythm track of Verne & Sons 'Little Boy Blue'. The record was released under the name of Judge Dread in honour of a character from Prince Buster. The record eventually took the charts by storm despite no air play as the BBC had banned the record. Trojan's devious attempts to convince otherwise that the record was not rude fell on the same deaf ears that had banned 'Wet Dream' some three years earlier. The ban did not prevent the record becoming a chart hit following in the footsteps of Max Romeo's chart success in 1969. 'Big Six' peaked at number 11 and featured on the chart for some six months, selling a very creditable 300,000 copies.

THE HISTORY OF SKINHEAD REGGAE 1968-1972 CHARTBUSTERS

THERE ARE MORE QUESTIONS THAN ANSWERS   JOHNNY NASH
Released on CBS   CBS S 8351   1972
Highest chart position   9   28/10/1972

The third of Johnny Nash's hits coming at the end of the golden era of reggae, mirroring his early success during the later end of the rocksteady period, His last offering featured on the chart for nine weeks as 1972 was drawing to an end.

6. GARY GLITTER – I DIDN'T KNOW I LOVED YOU (TILL I SAW YOU R
7. PETER SKELLERN – YOUR'E A LADY
8. ELVIS PRESLEY – BURNING LOVE
9. JOHNNY NASH – THERE ARE MORE QUESTIONS THAN ANSWERS
10. THE SWEET WIG-WAM BAM
11. THE CARPENTERS – GOODBYE TO LOVE

BIG SEVEN   JUDGE DREAD
Released on BIG SHOT   BI-613   1972
Highest chart position   18   30/12/1972

As night follows day 'Big Seven' followed 'Big Six' with another massive hit in the same vein, this time achieving greater chart success. 'Big Seven' was co-written with Rupie Edwards who had purchased a rhythm track from Bunny Lee. The track was previously released by the Uniques in 1968 titled 'My Conversation'. The backing track also featured as the rhythm for 'President Mash Up The Resident' by Shorty, a track that featured on 'Tighten Up Volume 6'. 'Big Seven' entered the charts whilst 'Big Six' was still selling well, with the Judge enjoying two chart entries for twelve weeks. Despite the inevitable ban the record sold well reaching number 8 in the following January having first entered the charts on the 9th of December 1972. 'Big Seven' featured on the chart for eighteen weeks with predictably Eight, Nine, Ten and One following in the same vein.

Looking back on the chart hits of 1968-1972 it was a remarkable period for reggae and Trojan in particular as they had issued twenty four of the twenty nine reggae records that made it into the top thirty. If we had counted 'Johnny Reggae' from The Piglets that would have completed a 'Top Thirty' thirty, the record making the lofty heights of number 3 on the 20th November 1971, released on BELL-1180 with the arrangement provided courtesy of Johnny Arthey.

Following the launch of BBC Radio One in September 1967 the chart was compiled from a combination of data from record shops collated by four music magazines including Record Mirror and Melody Maker. Concerns arose over the fixing of the charts, in the main by record promoters buying large quantities of a record at the targeted shops. This method was withdrawn in 1969. The British Market Research Bureau used a new method where every sale from 300 shops was recorded, the chart then compiled from a random selection of 150 of the outlets.

It seemed that the mainstream DJ's at the BBC refused to play the new Jamaican music on 'their' shows, reluctantly doing so when a song had made headway towards the charts. Accusations of 'patois lyrics' making the records indiscernible to the mainstream and the skinhead connection were said to have been reasons to shelve the music. The emerging Radio One had launched in the autumn of 67 and appeared hostile to reggae from the outset, all that was except for the main man, Emperor Rosko, who had fallen in love with and championed Jamaican music from the earlier days of blue beat and ska.

Emperor Rosko, born Michael Pasternak, in Los Angeles, California had arrived at the BBC following stints with Radio Caroline and Radio Luxembourg. The Emperor would produce his own shows and did not comply with the 'hits that were happening' and was able to feature a wider spectrum of music, including of course reggae. He built up a tremendous following with his Saturday slot always a programme awaited with anticipation by the skinheads and other music lovers of Motown and the new rock. Rosko became a reggae legend when he appeared on the cover of 'Club Reggae Volume 4' released on Trojan TBL 188 in 1972, and went on to cut his own version of Prince Buster's 'Alcapone' also released on Trojan later in the decade.

LESLIE KONG

The legendary producer Leslie Kong is credited to bringing reggae to the fore in the UK and without his influence the UK reggae scene would have been much poorer. He began his working life with his brothers running an ice cream parlour and record shop called Beverley's on Orange Street in Kingston.

It was on Orange Stree that he had a chance meeting with Jimmy Cliff for the first time in 1962. Jimmy was singing a song that he had written outside of Kong's shop, a meeting that led to Kong launching his own record label aptly named Beverley's. Jimmy Cliff's first record, the song he had been singing was issued on Beverley's, titled 'Dearest Beverley', a song that launched his distinguished career.

That same year Leslie Kong also recorded Bob Marley's first ever singles 'One Cup Of Coffee' and 'Judge Not' and Jimmy Cliff's massive Jamaican hit 'Miss Jamaica'. Leslie Kong soon built himself a reputation as Jamaica's foremost producer. He became known as the Chinaman and through the evolvement of ska to rocksteady then reggae he worked with some of the best artists including Desmond Dekker and Toots & The Maytals. A shrewd businessman he set up a deal with Island's Chris Blackwell in 1963 to issue work on the Black Swan label.

When Blackwell eventually bought out Kong's shares in Island Kong established a new partnership with Graeme Goodall's Pyramid label. When Pyramid closed down in 1969 Kong set up a licensing agreement with Trojan Records.

Leslie Kong was the first Jamaican producer to achieve an international hit in 1967 with Desmond Dekker's '007 (Shanty Town)' reaching number 14 on the UK chart. It would however be the 1968 release originally titled 'Poor Me Israelites' but shortened to 'Israelites' for the UK market that brought him truly international acclaim.

'Israelites' hit the number one spot on the British chart in April 1969, a massively popular record with the up-and-coming skinheads and the West Indians, selling over two million copies worldwide and for many their first introduction to reggae.

Other quality recordings originating from his studios were The Pioneers 'Long Shot Kick De Bucket', The Maytals '54-46 That's My Number' and their popular hit 'Monkey Man', a record that incidentally gained a UK chart entry at number 42 in 1970.

Leslie Kong was a talented producer who would only employ the best musicians with his session band known as The Beverley Allstars. Artists who had recorded at Beverley's include Peter Tosh, Ken Boothe, Bruce Ruffin and The Gaylads. The acclaimed film released in 1972, 'The Harder They Come' saw Leslie Kong in a cameo appearance as the producer overseeing a recording session with Toots & The Maytals, whilst Ivan (Jimmy Cliff) watches on in awe.

It is well documented that Leslie Kong died of a heart attack in August 1971 prior to the release of the film in the UK. His death, it has been said many times, had a devastating effect of the future work of many artists.

LEE 'SCRATCH' PERRY

Lee 'Scratch' Perry was born Rainford Hugh Perry on the 20th march 1936 in Kendal, a small town close to the centre of Jamaica. One of the major influential figures in the emerging world of reggae, producer 'Scratch' is best known as The Upsetter. His musical career can be traced as far back as 1959 when he formed an association with Clement 'Coxone' Dodd's sound system, initially as a record seller.

He progressed to supervising auditions at Dodd's shop located on Orange Street, Kingston although his relationship with Dodd was described as sometimes turbulent. During his time as a producer in the early sixties, although he was never credited on the records, he also recorded some work of his own.

The situation worsened with Dodd, due it was said to personal and financial problems and he moved to Joe Gibbs Amalgamated Records. 1968 saw Perry continued recording but problems soon surfaced again and he left Gibbs to form his own label, Upsetter.

His first single 'People Funny Boy' credited to Lee 'King' Perry was released on Doctor Bird DB-1146 being aimed as an insult to Gibbs, selling a remarkable 60,000 copies in Jamaica. The record carried what was described as a fast chugging beat, a change from the slower rocksteady, a beat that soon became identifiable as reggae.

The record was popular with the emerging skinheads who had bought previous Lee Perry recordings from 1968 including David Isaacs 'Place In The Sun' and The Untouchables 'Tighten Up' both tracks appearing later on Trojan's early compilation series 'Tighten Up', an album that retailed for just 14/6d. Tighten Up would become an integral part of the skinheads collection and the forerunner for Trojan's 'Club Reggae' and 'Reggae Chartbusters' series.

From 1968 through to 1972 Perry continued to release numerous recordings on several different labels including the UK Upsetter label, a subsidiary of Trojan that saw chart success for the Upsetters in 1969 with 'Return Of Django'. The record peaked at number 5 in the top 30 where it remained for three weeks during November that year, spending a creditable fifteen weeks on the chart. One of the follow up releases 'Clint Eastwood' flirted just outside but never quite made the charts, released on Pama's Punch label.

The UK charts looked like this on the 15th November 1969:

1. Archies - Sugar Sugar
2. Fleetwood Mac - Oh Well
3. The Tremoloes - (Call Me) Number One
4. The Hollies - He Ain't Heavy He's My Brother
5. Upsetters - Return Of Django / Dollar In The Teeth
6. The Beatles - Something / Come Together
7. Jimmy Cliff - Wonderful World Beautiful People
8. Frank Sinatra - Love's Been Good To Me
9. Karen Young - Nobody's Child
10. Lou Christie - I'm Gonna Make You Mine

Between 1968 and 1972 no fewer than six albums were produced by Perry during that time. Without doubt the most famous group ever to emerge from Jamaica, Bob Marley and The Wailers, who had worked with Perry, released several tracks during 1970 through to 1972. Most notable of these were, 'Duppy Conqueror' released on Upsetter UPS-348, 'My Cup' released on Upsetter UPS-340, 'Down Presser' released on Punch PH-77, 'Small Axe' Upsetter UPS-357 and 'Keep On Moving' Upsetter UPS-392.

DUPPY CONQUEROR

Produced by Lee Perry during 1970 and released on UPSETTER US-348 'Duppy Conqueror' was said to have been written by Bob Marley as a consequence of Bob complaining to Lee that he was too successful and was being plagued by hangers on, referring to them as Duppies. A Duppy in Jamaican folklore is a ghost, a wicked supernatural being, and Lee is reported to have said to Bob, that he could sort it out as they are Duppy Conquerors, with Bob proceeding to write the song.

THE HISTORY OF SKINHEAD REGGAE 1968-1972   LEE 'SCRATCH' PERRY

THE UPSETTER   TROJAN RECORDS TTL 13
Released 1969

Side
1. TIDAL WAVE 2. HEAT PROOF 3. TO LOVE SOMEBODY
4. NIGHT DOCTOR 5. SOULFUL I 6. BIG NOISE

Side 2
1. MAN FROM M.I.5 2. DREAD LUCK 3. KIDDY O
4. WOLF MAN 5. CRYING ABOUT YOU 6. THUNDERBALL

RETURN OF DJANGO TROJAN (UPSETTER)   TRLS 19
Released 1970

Side 1
1. RETURN OF DJANGO 2. TOUCH OF FIRE 3. COLD SWEAT
4. DRUGS AND POISON 5. SOULFUL I 6. NIGHT DOCTOR

Side 2
1. ONE PUNCH 2. EIGHT FOR EIGHT 3. LIVE INJECTION
4. MAN FROM M.I.5 5. TEN TO TWELVE 6. MEDICAL OPERATION

THE HISTORY OF SKINHEAD REGGAE 1968-1972   LEE 'SCRATCH' PERRY

SCRATCH THE UPSETTER AGAIN
TROJAN RECORDS TTL 28 Released 1970

Side 1
1. BAD TOOTH   2. THE DENTIS' (AKA THE DENTIST)   3. OUTER SPACE
4. ONE PUNCH   5. WILL YOU STILL LOVE ME   6. TAKE ONE

Side 2
1. SOUL WALK   2. I WANT TO THANK YOU
3. MULE TRAIN   Count Prince Miller
4. TOUCH OF FIRE   5. SHE IS GONE AGAIN   Alva Lewis
6. THE RESULT

EASTWOOD RIDES AGAIN
TROJAN RECORDS   TBL 125 Released   1970

Side 1
1. EASTWOOD RIDES AGAIN   2. HIT ME
3. KNOCK ON WOOD The Untouchables
4. POP CORN   5. CATCH THIS   6. YOU ARE ADORABLE   7. CAPSOL

Side 2
1. POWER PACK   2. DOLLAR IN THE TEETH   3. BABY BABY   Val Bennett
4. DJANGO   5. RED HOT   6. SALT AND PEPPER   7. TIGHT SPOT

The Upsetters had two albums released on the PAMA label during 1970.

CLINT EASTWOOD
PAMA RECORDS PSP 1014 1970

Side 1
1. RETURN OF THE UGLY 2. FOR A FEW DOLLARS MORE
3. PRISONER OF LOVE 4. DRY ACID 5. RIGHTFUL RULER
6. CLINT EASTWOOD

Side 2
1. TASTE OF KILLING 2. SELASSIE 3. WHAT IS THIS ?
4. NEVER FOUND ME A GIRL 5. MY MOB 6. CAUGHT YOU

MANY MOODS OF THE UPSETTERS
PAMA RECORDS SECO 24 1970

Side 1
1. EX - RAY VISION 2. CAN'T TAKE IT ANYMORE
3. SOUL STEW 4. LOW LIGHT 5. CLOUD NINE 6. BEWARE

Side 2
1. SERIOUS JOKE 2. GOOSEY 3. PROVE IT 4. BOSS SOCIETY
5. MEAN & DANGEROUS 6. GAMES PEOPLE PLAY

HARRY JOHNSON (HARRY J)

Harry Zephaniah Johnson, better known as Harry J, was born on July 6th 1945 in Westmoreland, Jamaica. His early success as a producer came with the golden age of reggae.

His first introduction to the music business was playing the bass with a group called the Virtues but he soon moved on to a stint as an insurance salesman. On returning to the music industry his first work as a record producer came in 1968 when he launched his own record label, Harry J. The first release was the Beltones, 'No More Heartaches' considered by many to be one of the first reggae songs ever recorded at the same time as Studio One produced 'Nanny Goat' by Larry & Alvin. Coxone Dodd had allowed Johnson to use the facilities at Studio One.

1969 brought international success with his hit 'Liquidator' TR-675 reaching number 9 in the UK chart in November, a very popular tune and a record that would become a popular anthem with the emerging skinheads. The track would be later used as the introduction on a hit for the Staple Singers, 'I'll Take You There'. An album followed aptly titled 'Liquidator' by Harry J All-stars issued on the Harry J label with a Trojan prefix TBL 104 in 1969.

Further chart success followed in 1970 with the massive hit for the vocal duo Bob And Marcia with 'Young Gifted And Black' HJ-6605 reaching a commendable number 5 in the UK in April 1970. The UK hit was a strings added version of their original Jamaican recording.

In 1972 he sold his record shop to set up his own studio on Roosevelt Avenue, Kingston, Jamaica. The Harry J Studio would later become a recording Mecca for many artists including Bob Marley And The Wailers and The Rolling Stones.

Chris Blackwell the founder of Island Records spent a great deal of time at Harry J's before moving to England and it was to here that Blackwell sent Bob Marley to record the classic album 'Catch A Fire'. The studio also featured in the reggae movie 'Rockers'.

The UK chart of the 29th November 1969 was a high spot in the golden age of reggae and a money spinner for Trojan with three records riding high in the top ten. 'Liquidator' would spend a total of twenty weeks on the chart roller coasting then enjoying somewhat of brief resurgence rising back up the chart to reach number 10 in January 1970.

1. Archies - Sugar Sugar
2. The Tremeloes - (Call Me) Number One
3. Stevie Wonder - Yester-Me Yester-You Yesterday
4. Fleetwood Mac - Oh Well
5. Kenny Rogers - Ruby Don't Take Your Love To Town
6. The Beatles - Something / Come Together
7. **Jimmy Cliff - Wonderful World Beautiful People**
8. **Upsetters - Return Of Django / Dollar In The Teeth**
9. **Harry J All Stars - Liquidator**
10. Jethro Tull - Sweet Dream

SINGLES PRODUCED BY HARRY J 1968 – 1972

TROJAN (ISSUED ON HARRY J LABEL)

HJ-675 Liquidator   Harry J All-stars   1969
HJ-693 Put A Little Love In Your Heart   Marcie Griffiths   1969
HJ-694 Spyrone   Harry J All-stars   1969

HARRY J

HJ-6601 The Big Three   Harry J All-stars   1970
HJ-6602 The Dog   Harry J All-stars   1970
HJ-6603 Feel A Little Better   Lloyd Parks   1970
HJ-6604 Fire Fire   The Jamaicans   1970

SINGLES PRODUCED BY HARRY J 1968 – 1972 (continued)

HJ-6605 Young Gifted And Black   Bob And Marcia   1970
HJ-6607 Jack The Ripper   The Jay Boys   1970
HJ-6608 Reach For The Sky   Harry J All-stars   1970
HJ-6609 Jay Moon Walk   The Jay Boys   1970
HJ-6610 Je T'Aime   The Jay Boys   1970
HJ-6611 Hang My Head   Bob Andy   1970
HJ-6612 Peace Of Mind   Bob Andy   1970
HJ-6613 Put A Little Love In Your Heart   Marcia Griffiths   1970
HJ-6614 Didn't I   The Cables   1970
HJ-6615 Got To Get Ourselves Together   Bob And Marcia   1970
HJ-6616 Salt Of The Earth   The Cables   1970
HJ-6617 Del Gago   The Jay Boys   1970
HJ-6618 I Can't Get Next To You   The Jay Boys   1970
HJ-6619 Cambodia   The Blake Boys   1970
HJ-6620 Feel Alright   The Cables 1970
HJ-6621 Return Of The Liquidator   Harry J All-stars   1970
HJ-6623 Band Of Gold   Marcia Griffiths   1970
HJ-6624 The Same Old Life   Roy Panton   1970
HJ-6625 More Heartaches   Lizzie   1970
HJ-6626 Holy Moses   The Jay Boys   1970
HJ-6628 The Arcade Walk   The Jay Boys   1971
HJ-6631 United We Stand   Bob Andy And Marcia Griffiths   1971
HJ-6634 Set Me Free   Uriel Aldridge   1971
HJ-6640 Come Back And Stay   The Fabulous Five   1972
HJ-6641 Down Side Up   Carey & Lloyd   1972
HJ-6642 Skank In Bed   Bongo Herman & Les   1972

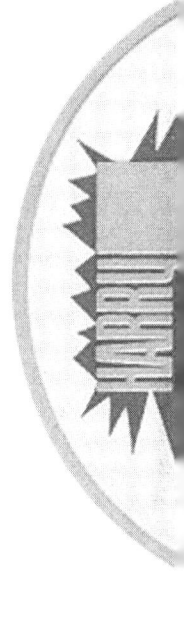

LIQUIDATOR HARRY J ALL STARS HARRY J TBL 104 1969
Side 1
1. JACK THE RIPPER 2. BIG THREE 3. MY CHERIE AMOUR
4. DON'T LET ME DOWN 5. LIQUIDATOR 6. SPYRONE

Side 2
1. REACH FOR THE SKY 2. INTERROGATOR 3. JAY MOON WALK
4. ELCONG 5. JE T'AIME 6. THE DOG

DANDY LIVINGSTONE SINGER/PRODUCER

Dandy Livingstone was born Robert Livingstone Thompson in Kingston, Jamaica on the 14th December 1943. He moved to England at the age of 15 at a time when many West Indians first came to Britain, seeking opportunities to better themselves and their children. Many had been recruited to overcome the shortage of workers particularly in transport and hospitals. Some were soldiers from the war that had only ceased a decade or so earlier, brave men who had fought for Britain during the 1939-1945 campaign.

Dandy's first record was somewhat of a surprise, being issued without him being aware. The single was a result of a jamming session with a friend. The record was released on the Planetone label in 1963. Whilst Livingstone was working in a record shop owned by Lee Gopthal, who later launched Trojan Records, he discovered that a local record company, Carnival records, were looking for a Jamaican vocal duo. Livingstone filled both roles by double taking his own voice, and the records were issued with the credit going to the artist Sugar & Dandy. One single 'What A Life' released in 1964 on the Carnival label CV-7015 sold over 25,000 copies. Live performances would later feature Tito Simon as the other half of the duo.

The up and coming Trojan signed Livingstone in 1968 under the noses of Pama releasing their first two albums, 'Follow That Donkey' TRL 1 and 'Dandy Returns' TRL 2. Robert Thomson being a man of many talents moved into production in 1968, a year that saw him team up with Audrey Hall, recording as Dandy & Audrey. As with other producers Trojan set up a subsidiary label, Downtown, to release Livingstone's work as singer and producer. The label was superseded by J-Dan from early 1970.

His productions included work for The Marvels and a single for Nicky Thomas, ironically titled 'Suzanne Beware Of The Devil', a record that brought Thompson chart success towards the end of 1972. He also produced 'Red Red Wine' for Tony Tribe, a hugely popular single with the growing band of skinheads, in 1969. Livingstone also worked with Rico Rodriguez who featured on the hit 'Rudy A Message To You' and produced several singles for Rodriguez under the name of Rico & The Rudies.

The single 'Reggae in Your Jeggae' was released on the Downtown label DT-410 in 1969 and became a popular offering amongst the skinheads. 'Version Girl' credited on the label to Boy Friday and produced by Dandy was a classic remake of Jackie Edwards 'What's Your Name' and was released on Downtown DT-470.

An album by Dandy & Audrey, 'Morning Side Of The Mountain', was issued on the Downtown label bearing the Trojan prefix TBL 118 during 1970.

By 1971 Thompson was becoming disillusioned with the music business and seemed to be losing direction so he moved to Jamaica as he was said to say at the time 'to recharge his musical batteries'. A year later he returned with new material and Trojan issued an album, but more important he had a new identity, he was now known as 'Dandy Livingstone'.

Several singles followed most notably recording as Boy Friday as the notes on 'Club Reggae Volume 2' mentioned , *The last year has seen the emergence of the 'Version' either being the instrumental of a vocal, or a record brought 'up to date' by dubbing the voice of a D.J. over the old tape. Examples of the latter are any U-Roy or Dennis Alcapone records, both noted for their fast talking rhymes using local slang and dialect, and thus quite often making the words completely unintelligible to an English audience. Producer Dandy gently satirizes the situation with his 'Version Girl' sung by Boy Friday, a relatively unknown singer whose voice sounds suspiciously familiar!*

Dandy Livingstone finally found chart Success in 1972 with 'Suzanne Beware Of The Devil' a single released on Trojan's Horse label, HOSS 16 reaching number 14 during October, one of the last three reggae records to feature in the charts during the golden age.

An album followed titled 'Dandy Livingstone' released on the more expensive Trojan series, TRLS 45.

The UK chart of the 7th October 1972 looked like this, and included Judge Dread with 'Big Six' at number 12 and Johnny Nash with his hit, 'More Questions Than Answers' featuring at number 26.

1. Davis Cassidy - How Can I Be Sure
2. T Rex - Children Of The Revolution
3. Lieutenant Pigeon - Mouldy Old Dough
4. The Sweet - Wig-Wam Bam
5. Donny Osmond - Too Young
6. Peter Skellern - Your A Lady
7. Slade - Mama Weer All Crazee Now
8. Gary Glitter - I Didn't Know You Loved Me (Till I Saw You Rock And Roll)
9. Faron Young - Four In The Morning
10. The Drifters - Come On Over To My Place (1972)
11. Elvis Presley - Burning Love
12. **Judge Dread - Big Six**
13. Michael Jackson - Ain't No Sunshine
14. **Dandy Livingstone - Suzanne Beware Of The Devil**

SINGLES DISCOGRAPHY 1968 – 1972

TROJAN
TR-601 Donkey Returns   Brother Dan All-stars   1968
TR-607 Read Up   Brother Dan All-stars   1968
TR-608 Another Saturday Night   Brother Dan All-stars   1968
TR-618 The Toast   Dandy   1968

DOWNTOWN
DT-401 Move Your Mule   Dandy   1968
DT-402 Come Back Girl   Dandy   1968
DT-404 Tell Me Darling   Brother Dan   1968
DT-405 Copy Your Rhythm   Brother Dan All-stars   1968
DT-406 Doctor Sure Shot   Dandy   1969
DT-410 Reggae In Your Jeggae   Dandy   1969
DT-413 Moma Moma   The Israelites   1969
DT-415 Rock Steady Gone   Dandy   1969
DT-416 I'm Your Puppet   Dandy   1969
DT-421 Games People Play   Dandy & Audrey   1969
DT-426 Everybody Feel Good   Downtown All-stars   1969
DT-429 People Get Ready   Dandy/The Rudies   1969
DT-433 Seven Books   The Israelites   1969
DT-434 Be Natural Be Proud   Dandy   1969
DT-437 Come On Home   Dandy   1969
DT-441 Burial Of Long Shot (Part 1)   Prince OF Darkness   1969
DT-442 Everybody Loves A Winner   Dandy   1969
DT-445 Come Together   The Israelites   1969
DT-447 Music Doctor   The Music Doctors   1969
DT-448 Meeting Over Yonder   Prince Of Darkness   1969
DT-450 Skinheads A Message To You   Desmond Riley   1969
DT-456 Raining In My Heart   Dandy   1970
DT-458 Build Your Heart On A Solid Foundation   Dandy   1970
DT-462 Morning Side Of The Mountain   Dandy & Audrey   1970
DT-470 Version Girl   Boy Friday   1970
DT-471 Music So Good   Boy Friday   1970
DT-473 Take A Message Rudy   Boy Friday   1970

J-DAN
JDN-4403 Bush Doctor   The Music Doctors   1970
JDN-4404 Preaching Love   The Music Doctors   1970
JDN-4410 Can't Help From Crying   The Israelites   1970
JDN-4411 The Wild Bunch   The Music Doctors   1970
JDN-4414 In The Summertime   The Music Doctors   1970

TROJAN
TR-7800 Take A Letter Maria   Dandy   1970
TR-7816 Same Old Fashioned Way   Dandy   1971

J-DAN
JDN-4416 I Don't Want No More   Boy Friday   1971
JDN-4417 Discretion Version   The Music Doctors   1971
JDN-4418 Situation Version   Boy Friday   1971

DOWNTOWN
DT-476 There'll Always Be Sunshine   Boy Friday   1971
DT-477 Hot Pants   Boy Friday   1971

TROJAN
TR-7828 Salt Of The Earth   Dandy   1971

DOWNTOWN
DT-480 The Pliers   The Music Doctors   1971
DT-481 El Raunchy   Boy Friday   1971
DT-483 Could It Be True   Dandy & Jackie   1971
DT-484 Daddy's Home   Dandy   1971
DT-489 Give Me Some More   Studio Sound   1972

HORSE
HOSS-16 Suzanne Beware Of The Devil   Dandy Livingstone   1972
HOSS-25 Big City   Dandy Livingstone   1972

TROJAN
TR-7857 What Do You Wanna Make Those Eyes At Me For?   Dandy Livingstone   1972

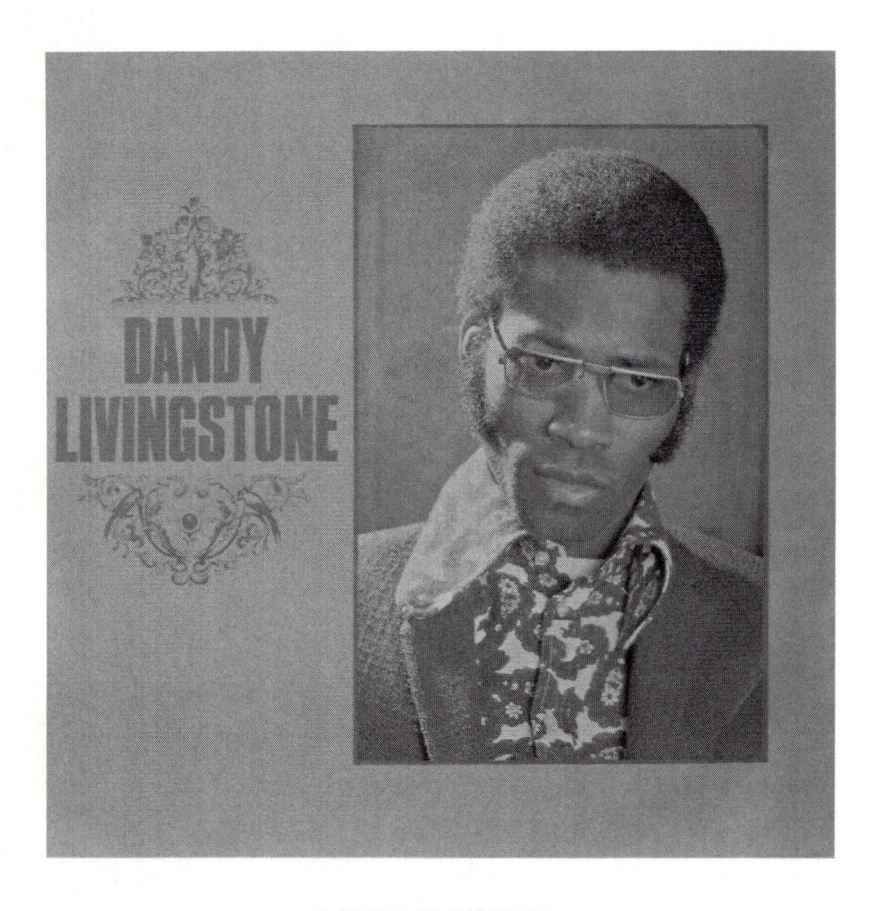

DANDY LIVINGSTONE
TROJAN RECORDS   TRLS 45   Released 1972

Side 1
1. BIG CITY   2. MAKE ME YOUR NUMBER ONE
3. WAR ACROSS THE NATION
4. WHAT DO YOU WANNA MAKE THOSE EYES AT ME FOR
5. THINK ABOUT THAT   6. SUNSHINE GIRL

Side 2
1. JAMAICA IS FUN   2. BRAND NEW DAY   3. AT THE CLUB
4. CONFIDENTIAL   5. DON'T BREAK YOUR PROMISE

CLANCY ECCLES PRODUCER/ARTIST

Clancy Eccles was brought up in the Parish of Saint Mary, Jamaica the son of a tailor and builder. Early in his life he would be influenced by spiritual music in church and grow to love singing. Clancy's musical career began with a stint working on the north coast hotel circuit, eventually moving to Ocho Rios. His big musical break like many of his contemporaries would come when he moved to Kingston and took part in a talent show, this one organized by Coxone Dodd. Clancy's early success featured several ska hits including 'River Jordon' and 'Sammy No Dead'.

Clancy then launched a series of talent shows of his own and began to organise concerts including amongst many The Wailers in the mid sixties. He left the music industry in 1965 to follow his father's profession as a tailor for a short time before returning to the music business in 1967. This time around though saw Clancy producing his own recordings as well as other artists.

Clancy Eccles was influential during the period of the hardening of rocksteady into reggae and has been credited as being the originator of the word 'reggae', derived from 'streggae', a word used in Kingston to describe a woman of the streets. The claim is emphasized in 'Bag A Boo' (Don't You Brag And Don't You Boast) a B side of The Slickers 'Auntie Lulu' released in 1969 on the Duke label.

However before 'Bag A Boo' his first hit in the UK was 'What Will Your Mama Say' released on Pama PM-701. In 1968 the skinheads adopted Clancy's 'Fattie Fattie' released on Trojan TR-658. The record became a classic skinhead track, although the lyrics to this day remain somewhat of a mystery. Along with 'Fattie Fattie' and 'Fire Corner' DU-30 released through Trojan on the Duke label some of his other production work also found favour with the skinheads, including 'Herbman Shuffle' from the legendary DJ King Stitt.

Clancy's session band The Dynamites recorded numerous instrumentals with many featuring as the B side to Clancy's singles. Clandisc a subsidiary of Trojan was launched in 1969 for the UK production of Clancy's own and his artists work. The label soon grew a reputation for quality releases including, 'Holly Holy' by The Fabulous Flames and 'Sweet Jamaica' sung admirably by Clancy, both outstanding tracks.

Both tracks went on to feature on Trojan's 'Club Reggae' Volume 1 and Volume 2 respectfully. Clancy had built a reputation of fairness and a sense of equality and helped fellow musicians including Lee 'Scratch' Perry set up his own label in 1968. Clancy Eccles died on the 30th June 2005 in Spanish Town Hospital, Jamaica as a result of a heart attack.

SELECTED DISCOGRAPHY SINGLES 1968-1972

DOCTOR BIRD
DB-1156 Feel The Rhythm 1968

CLANDISC
CLA-201 The World Needs Loving 1969
CLA-202(B) Mount Zion 1969
CLA-220(B) Dance Beat 1969

DUKE
DU-9(B) Bag A Boo 1969
DU-30 Fire Corner 1969

TROJAN
TR-639 Sweet Africa 1969
TR-647 Bangarang Crash 1969
TR-658 Fattie Fattie 1969

CLANDISC
CLA-214 Africa 1970
CLA-221 Unite Tonight 1970
CLA-235 John Crow Skank 1971

TROJAN
TR-7815(B) Credit Squeeze 1971

CLANDISC
CLA-239 Hallelujah Free At Last 1972

FREEDOM TROJAN RECORDS TTL 22
Issued on CLANDISC Released 1969

Side 1
1. FREEDOM 2. WHAT WILL YOUR MOTHER SAY
3. TWO OF A KIND 4. THE WORLD NEEDS LOVING
5. DOLLAR TRAIN 6. CONSTANTINOPLE

Side 2
1. FATTIE FATTIE 2. AUNTIE LULU 3. SHU BE DU
4. MY GIRL 5. I NEED YOU 6. MOUNTZION

ERIC DONALDSON

The very successful singer-songwriter Eric Donaldson was born in St. Catherine, Jamaica on the 11th June 1947. He attended school in Spanish Town before taking a job as a painter, always singing in his spare time and during his late teens he cut some un-released tracks for Studio One. The mid sixties saw him form a vocal group, The West Indians, with their first Jamaican hit coming in 1968 with 'Right Time', a track produced by JJ Johnson.

The group also recorded for Lee 'Scratch' Perry, changing their name to the 'Killowatts'. However no real success could be found and the group broke up in 1970. Donaldson then cut some tracks for Alvin Ranglin's GG Label including 'Lonely Night' then for Dynamic Studios a track called 'Never Gonna Give You Up' but neither found favour at the time.

In 1971 as a last stand Eric entered the Festival Song Competition with 'Cherry Oh Baby'. It was said by many at the time from the first rehearsals that those present knew they were listening to the winner. From that day Eric Donaldson will forever be associated with the Jamaican Festival Song Competition and in particular, for his winning entry, a song recorded by many since but never equalled, sung in his trademark falsetto voice, a triumph that launched his career.

It has been reported that when he first came out on stage at the famous State Theatre for the final competition shouts of 'go away country man' could be heard. Then he began to sing and before the first line was completed it was bedlam, people in the front rows rushed on stage lifted him to their shoulders and proclaimed him even then as one of the biggest superstars to hit Jamaica in a long while.

An album was recorded at Dynamic Studios and released toward the end of 1971 on Byron Lee's subsidiary label, Jaguar. The album 'Eric Donaldson' sold an extraordinary 50,000 copies. Seven of the tracks were Donaldson's original compositions, including 'Cherry Oh Baby' and 'Miserable Woman' with a cover of 'Love of the Common People' included. Trojan in due course released the album in the UK during 1972 on TRLS 42.

Eric Donaldson soon became a household name in Jamaica although chart success in the UK eluded him, nonetheless outstanding reggae singles, should not and never were measured on chart success.

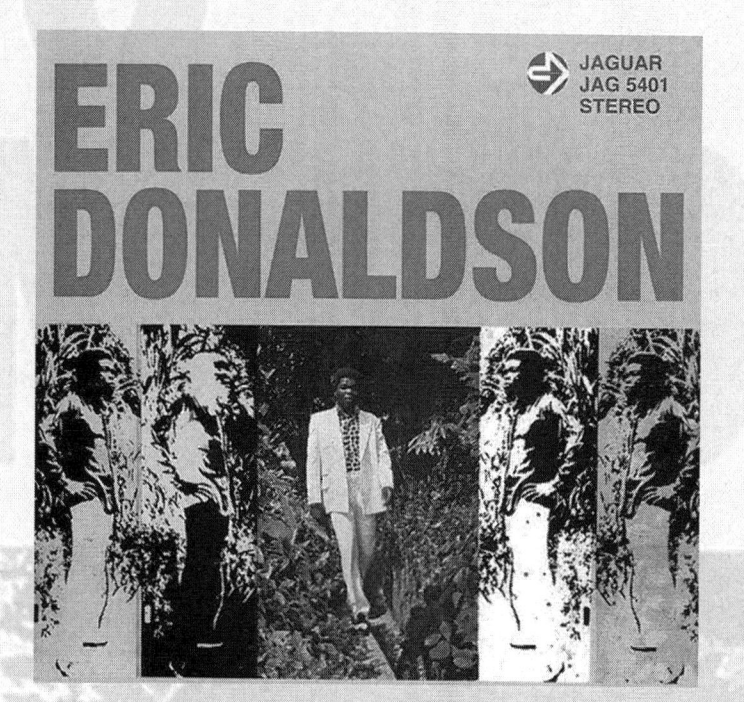

ERIC DONALDSON   ERIC DONALDSON

JAGUAR RECORDS Jamaican release 1971
TROJAN RECORDS TRLS 42 Released 1972

Side 1
1. CHERRY OH BABY   2. MISERABLE WOMAN
3. GOT TO GET YOU OFF MY MIND
4. PLEASE LET ME LOVE YOU
5. GO AWAY

Side 2
1. LOVE OF THE COMMON PEOPLE   2. NEVER ON A SUNDAY
3. JUST CAN'T HAPPEN THIS WAY   4. BUILD MY WORLD
5. THE LION SLEEPS

THE HISTORY OF SKINHEAD REGGAE 1968-1972   ERIC DONALDSON

Cherry Oh Baby
Eric Donaldson

CHERRY OH BABY featured as the opening track on the successful Trojan 'Club Reggae Volume 2' TBL 164 released in 1971

SELECTED SINGLES DISCOGRAPHY 1968-1972

DYNAMIC
DYN-420 Cherry, Oh Baby 1971
DYN-425 Just Can't (Happen This Way) 1971
DYN-439 Miserable Woman 1972
DYN-445 Blue Boot 1972
DYN-452 Little Did You Know 1972

DENNIS ALCAPONE

Dennis Alcapone was born Dennis Smith on the 6th August 1947 in Clarendon Jamaica but moved to Kingston from a very early age. Dennis began his working life as a welder for the Jamaican Public Services by day, but his nights were spent at the various sound systems of the time, including those run by Coxone Dodd, Duke Reid and Prince Buster.

He set up his own small Hi Fi sound system El Paso with two friends and was soon spotted by producer Keith Hudson who liked his sharp talking over the records of the day. The founder of the Deejay or Toaster was Ewart Beckford, better known as Hugh Roy who began talking over Duke Reid rocksteady tracks and was seen as the Daddy of talk over but Dennis Alcapone came very close. His first recording was under the title of Dennis Smith. He joined Clement Dodd's Studio One as the legendary Hugh Roy or U.Roy was well established with Duke Reid as his number one deejay.

His debut single for Dodd 'Nanny Version' was an instant hit in Jamaica with his talk over revamping an old song, it was also the first record to be credited to Dennis Alcapone. That first record had many convinced that it was in fact U.Roy but it soon became apparent that Alcapone's voice was clearer and more distinct and became the sound the youth wanted to hear.

Dennis found considerable chart success in Jamaica and topped the charts with several singles including 'Guns Don't Argue' AKA 'Alcapone Guns Don't Bark' and 'Ripe Cherry' both using backing tracks of fellow studio artist Eric Donaldson's 'Love Of The Common People' and 'Cherry Oh Baby' respectively. 'Guns Don't Bark' would feature on Trojan's 'Club Reggae Volume 3' and 'Ripe Cherry' found its way onto their 'Tighten Up Volume 5'.

During 1971 Dennis joined forces with his old friend Bunny Lee releasing 'It Must Come' utilising 'Better Must Come' as the backing track and 'Cherry Oh Baby' featured again on another track this time produced by Lee 'Scratch' Perry. 'Well Dread' was originally to have been voiced by Lizzy but Perry decided that Dennis should voice it himself.

An inevitable album followed, originally released in Jamaica in 1971 on the Jaguar label. The same album was released in the UK on Trojan in 1972, appropriately titled 'Guns Don't Argue' TBL 187.

GUNS DON'T ARGUE   DENNIS ALCAPONE   TROJAN TBL 187 1972

Side 1
1. ALCAPONES GUNS DON'T ARGUE   2. IT MUST COME
3. AIN'T TOO PROUD TO BEG   4. EVERYBODY NEEDS LOVE
5. IF IT DON'T WORK OUT

Side 2
1. TEACHER TEACHER   2. LEFT WITH A BROKEN HEART
3. YOU GOT WHAT IT TAKES   4. WORLD WIDE LOVE
5. SOMEONE DANCING WITH MY GIRL

SINGLES DISCOGRAPHY 1970-1972

ACKEE
ACK-114 Happy Go Lucky Girl 1970

BANANA
BA-324 Nanny Version 1970

CAMEL
CA-56 Everybody Bawlin 1970

SUPREME
SUP-214 You Must Believe Me 1970

BANANA
BA-326 Home Version 1971
BA-328 Duppy Serenade 1971
BA-341 Forever Version 1971

BIG SHOT
BI-565 Shades Of Hudson 1971
BI-572 Out De Light Baby 1971

CAMEL
CA-74 This A Butter 1971

DUKE
DU-125 Medley Version 1971

DYNAMIC
DYN-421 Horse And Buggy 1971
DYN-422 Ripe Cherry 1971
DYN-427 Alcapone's Guns Don't Bark 1971

EXPLOSION
EX-2039 Revelation Version 1971

G.G.
GG-4526 King Of Kings 1971

JACKPOT
JP-773 Jumping Jack 1971
JP-775 Togetherness 1971
JP-776 Tell It Like It Is 1971

TROPICAL
AL-003 False Prophet 1971

UPSETTER
US-373 Well Dread 1971
US-377 Alpha And Omega 1971

ACKEE
ACK-146 Power Version 1972

ATTACK
ATT-8027 Fine Style 1972

BULLET
BU-509 Dup-Up A Daughter 1972

DOWNTOWN
DT-496 Swinging Along 1972

DUKE
DU-131 The Sky's The Limit 1972
DU-147 Get In The Groove 1972

DUKE REID
DR-2520 Rock To The Beat (Number One Station) 1972

G.G.
GG-4538 Musical Alphabet 1972

GRAPE
GR-3035 Rasta Dub 1972

GREEN DOOR
GD-4041 Rub Up A Daughter 1972

TECHNIQUES
TE-918 Look Into Yourself 1972

TREASURE ISLE
TI-7069 The Great Woggie 1972
TI-7071 Judgement Day (with Hopeton Lewis) 1972

UPSETTER
US-381 Wonderman 197
US-388 Master Key 1972
US-389 Back Biter 1972

U.ROY or HUGH ROY

U.Roy also known as Hugh Roy was born Ewart Beckford in Jones Town, Jamaica on the 21st September 1942. Reggae's greatest deejay also known as 'The Originator' found recognition in the late 60s and early 70s with a string of hits. He is famed as the inventor of 'Toasting', using vocal improvisation and rapping over previously released popular songs.

His musical career began back in 1961 as a deejay at several of the sound systems of the day including Coxone Dodd's number two set whilst King Stitt known as 'The Ugly One' ran his number one station; sounds a familiar lyric. Working with Duke Reid gave Hugh Roy access to Treasure Isles vast back catalogue of hits to experiment with and although not the first deejay to talk over an old hit he was the first to find fame through his recording techniques, he didn't just talk over he wrote a 'riddim' from start to finish ending up with a polished track.

Working alongside Duke Reid they created 'Wear You To The Ball', a record previously a hit for The Paragons in the 60s now getting a new lease of life and a huge hit in Jamaica for Hugh Roy and John Holt. John Holt was the lead singer with The Paragons and had become a huge fan of Hugh Roy as he was known at that time.

The hits began to come with 'Wear You To The Ball' released on Duke Reid DR-2513 in 1970 kicking it all off. Next up was 'You'll Never Get Away' Duke Reid DR-2514 and 'Version Galore', also released on the Duke Reid label DR-2515. U.Roy worked with most of the top Jamaican producers including Bunny Lee, Lee 'Scratch' Perry, Sonia Pottinger and Alvin Ranglin. An album was released in the UK in 1971 on Trojan, TBL 161 titled 'Version Galore'.

Included on the album were several re workings of the classic hits from The Paragons. 'On The Beach' and "The Tide Is High' featured, a track incidentally that provided a huge number one hit for Blondie in 1980 on both side of the Atlantic, although many at the time did not realise its provenance. Other tracks attributed to the Paragons on the album were 'Happy Go Lucky Girl' and of course 'Wear You To The Ball', a record that had made it onto Trojan's first in the series of 'Club Reggae' issued the same year.

1972 saw the release on Pama prefix PM-835 of 'Way Down South', produced by Alvin Ranglin, the track a version of 'Take Warning' by Billy Dyce also featured as the B side on Trojan's GG label GG-4532 and made it onto Pama's 'Straighten Up Volume 3' album both released the same year.

1972 heralded the release on Trojan of a second album in the Version series 'Version Galore volume 2' TBL 175. Although this time the album featured tracks by one of his deejay compatriots, the up and coming Dennis Alcapone, of whom it has already been said had a clearer style that endeared him greatly to the youth and in particular the remaining skinheads.

VERSION GALORE   TROJAN RECORDS TBL 161   Released 1971

SELECTED SINGLES DISCOGRAPHY 1970-1972

DUKE REID
DU-2513 Wear You To The Ball   Hugh Roy And John Holt   1970
DU-2514 You'll Never Get Away   Hugh Roy   1970
DU-2515 Version Galore   Hugh Roy   1970

DUKE
DU-105 Love I Tender   Hugh Roy   1970

UNITY
UN-568(B) Wake The Nation   Jeff Barnes & Hugh Roy   1970

DUKE REID
DR-2509 Wake The Town   Hugh Roy   1970
DR-2510 Rule The Nation   Hugh Roy   1970
DR-2517 Tom Drunk   U-Roy & Hopeton Lewis   1971
DR-2518 True True   Hugh Roy   1971
DR-2519 Flashing My Whip   Hugh Roy   1971
DR 2520 Rock To The Beat   U.Roy   1972

DYNAMIC
DYN-488 Festival Wise   Hugh Roy   1972

GRAPE
GR-3026 On Top Of The Peak   U.Roy   1972

TROJAN
TR-7884 Hat Trick C/W Wet Vision   U.Roy   1972

PAMA
PM-835 Way Down South   Hugh Roy   1972

BOB MARLEY AND THE WAILERS

The renowned group was lead by Bob Marley who was born Nesta Robert Marley in the village of Nine Mile in the parish of St. Anne, Jamaica on the 6th February 1945. His father was a white Jamaican of English descent. It is understood that a Jamaican passport official inadvertently swapped his first and middle names.

Bob Marley passed away on the 11th May 1981 having become the first truly international reggae super star. The Wailers had begun life in 1963 formed by Bob Marley, Peter Tosh and Bunny Wailer. Their original recordings were under the guise of The Wailing Wailers later changing their name to The Wailers.

Their early recordings were of an exceptional standard; just listen if you can to 'Simmer Down' and 'Shame And Scandal'. In 1967 The Wailers started their own record label and released their first singles including 'Nice Time' and 'Stir It Up' a track penned by Bob for his wife Rita. The label soon folded and Bob began writing songs for Johnny Nash including amongst many 'Guava Jelly'.

1970 through to 1972 saw the groups recordings produced by Lee 'Scratch' Perry with the most notable tracks released on a variety of labels including 'Guava Jelly' on Trojan's Green Door GD-4025 and 'Small Axe' on Perry's Trojan subsidiaries Upsetter label US-357 with 'Lively Up Yourself' issued on the charismatic Pama Punch label PH-102. 'Stir It Up' was first popularised by the American singer Johnny Nash reaching number 13 on the UK charts in 1972.

The emerging reggae years in the UK of 1968 – 1972 were dominated by, and will always be remembered for groups like, The Pioneers, Greyhound, Toots And The Maytals, The Upsetters alongside Desmond Dekker, Jimmy Cliff, Nicky Thomas, Dave And Ansel Collins and Bob And Marcia.

Bob Marley And The Wailers had already enjoyed considerable success in Jamaica but in the UK were to some extent during this period in the shadows to the mainstream and never broke into the charts. During 1971 they were described as a group with fine harmonizing and controversial lyrics and their singles 'Small Axe' and 'Duppy Conqueror' featured on Trojan's 'Club Reggae Volume 2' and 'Tighten Up Volume 5' respectfully. Their time was to come and it was somewhat ironic that the break came with the departure of Jimmy Cliff from Island Records leaving Chris Blackwell looking for a talented replacement.

Bob who was stranded in the UK at the time whilst on tour walked into Blackwell's office and was subsequently offered £4,000 to record an album for Island back in Jamaica. 'Catch A Fire' was released later in 1973 and the rest they say is history. The album included 'Stir It Up' and established the band and in particular Bob Marley as international superstars who began a new transformation, resurrecting the sounds of Jamaica during the mid seventies, a sound they could truly call their own.

SMALL AXE UPSETTER US-357 1971

SINGLES DISCOGRAPHY 1968-1972

FAB
FAB-34 Pound Get A Blow   1968
FAB-36 Thank You Lord   1968
FAB-37 Nice Time   1968

TROJAN
TR-617 Stir It Up   1968

ESCORT
ERT- 842 To The Rescue   1970

UPSETTER
US-340 My Cup   1970
US-348 Duppy Conqueror   1970

BULLET
BU-493 Lick Samba   1971

GREEN DOOR
GD- 4005 Trench Town Rock   1971

PUNCH
PH-77 Down Presser   1971

UPSETTER
US-357 Small Axe   1971
US-371 Dreamland   1971
US-372 More Axe   1971

GREEN DOOR
GD-4025 Guava Jelly   1972

PUNCH
PH-101 Screw Face
PH-102 Lively Up Yourself   1972

UPSETTER
US-392 Keep On Moving   1972

THE HISTORY OF SKINHEAD REGGAE 1968-1972   BOB MARLEY AND THE WAILERS

DISCOGRAPHY 1968-1972 ALBUMS

SOUL REBEL   TROJAN RECORDS   TBL 126 1970

Side 1
1. SOUL REBEL
2. TRY ME   3. IT'S ALRIGHT
4. NO SYMPATHY   5. MY CUP
6. SOUL ALMIGHTY

Side 2
1. REBEL'S HOP   2. CORNER STONE
3. 400 YEARS   4. NO WATER
5. REACTION   6. MY SYMPATHY

SOUL REVOLUTION PART II UPSETTER TBL 65 1971

Side 1
1. KEEP ON MOVING   2. DON'T ROCK MY BOAT   3. PUT IT ON
4. FUSSING AND FIGHTING   5. DUPPY CONQUEROR   6. MEMPHIS

Side 2
1. RIDING HIGH   2. KAYA   3. AFRICAN HERBSMAN
4. STAND ALONE   5. SUN IS SHINING   6. BRAIN WASHING

SOUL REVOLUTION, the second Wailers album produced by Lee 'Scratch' Perry was originally released in a very limited edition, on the Jamaican Maroon label. SOUL REVOLUTION PART II was an interesting sequel, an album of pure rhythm tracks thought to be a first in Jamaican music.

JOHNNY NASH

Johnny Nash began his musical career as a pop singer in the late 1950s. He was born John Lester Nash Jr. in Houston, Texas, USA in 1940. As early as 1965 Johnny Nash had formed the JAD Record label in New York.

The reggae connection began during 1968 when Nash travelled to Jamaica and recorded several hits encouraged by the fact that his girlfriend had close family connections with the local radio and television host Neville Willoughby. His aim was to bring the rocksteady sound to America from Jamaica.

To help with this task Nash was introduced to a relatively young local group who were at the time struggling to make it in the music business called The Wailers. Bob Marley, Peter Tosh and Bunny Wailer introduced Nash to the local scene and all three were signed to an exclusive publishing deal with JAD, Nash financing some of their early work with Byron Lee's Dragonairies.

Johnny Nash enjoyed early success in the UK chart with the rocksteady releases 'Hold Me Tight' reaching number 5 in 1968 and 'You Got Soul' number 6 in January 1969 with a follow up release 'Cupid' matching the previous achievement in April the same year. Further chart success followed with 'Stir It Up' written by Bob Marley, released on CBS Records CBS-7800 peaking at number 13 in April 1972.

The single was taken from the album 'I Can See Clearly Now' recorded in London the same year, an album that included a further three tracks penned by Marley. 'Guava Jelly', 'Comma Comma' and 'You Poured Sugar on Me'.

The album sold over a million copies, and was awarded a gold disc in November 1972. The album yielded two further chart hits for Nash; the title track peaked at number 5 in June 1972 with a follow up 'There Are More Questions Than Answers' gaining a chart position the same year. Johnny Nash would continue to find chart success in the coming years.

The UK chart of the 29th April 1972 featured Johnny Nash with 'Stir it Up', Greyhound who had peaked at number 20 the same week and Paul Simon's 'Mother And Child Reunion' heading down the charts having achieved a creditable number 5 position during March.

13. **Johnny Nash - Stir It Up**
20. Greyhound - I Am What I Am
48. Paul Simon - Mother And Child Reunion

The UK chart of the 22nd July 1972 looked like this;

1. Donny Osmond - Puppy Love
2. Gary Glitter - Rock And Roll Parts 1 And 2
3. Dr Hook And The Medicine Show - Sylvia's Mother
4. The New Seekers - Circles
5. **Johnny Nash - I Can See Clearly Now**
6. The Sweet - Little Willy
7. The Partridge Family - Breaking Up Is Hard To Do
8. Slade - Take Me Back'Ome
9. The Who - Join Together
10. Elvis Presley - American Trilogy

Johnny Nash's next release 'There Are More Questions Than Answers' peaked at number 9 on the 28th October 1972, a chart that also saw Judge Dread feature with his 'Big Six' at number 15 on its way down from the lofty position of number 11 the previous week.

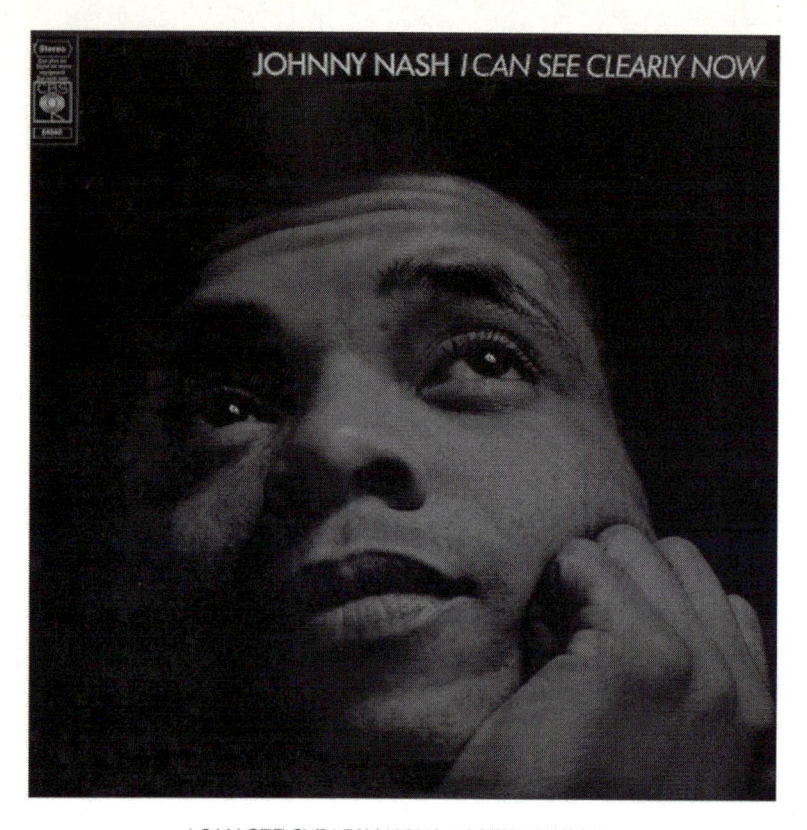

I CAN SEE CLEARLY NOW   JOHNNY NASH
CBS RECORDS   CBS S 64840   Released 1972

Side 1
1. STIR IT UP (R. Marley)   2. THAT'S THE WAY WE GET BY
3. GUAVA JELLY (R. Marley)   4. SO NICE WHILE IT LASTED
5. OOH BABY YOU'VE BEEN SO GOOD TO ME
6. YOU POURED SUGAR ON ME (R. Marley)

Side 2
1. I CAN SEE CLEARLY NOW   2. COMMA COMMA (R. Marley)
3. WE'RE ALL ALIKE   4. HOW GOOD IT IS
5. CREAM PUFF
(Original pressing featured THE FISH AND THE ALLEY OF DESTRUCTION)
6. THERE ARE MORE QUESTIONS THAN ANSWERS

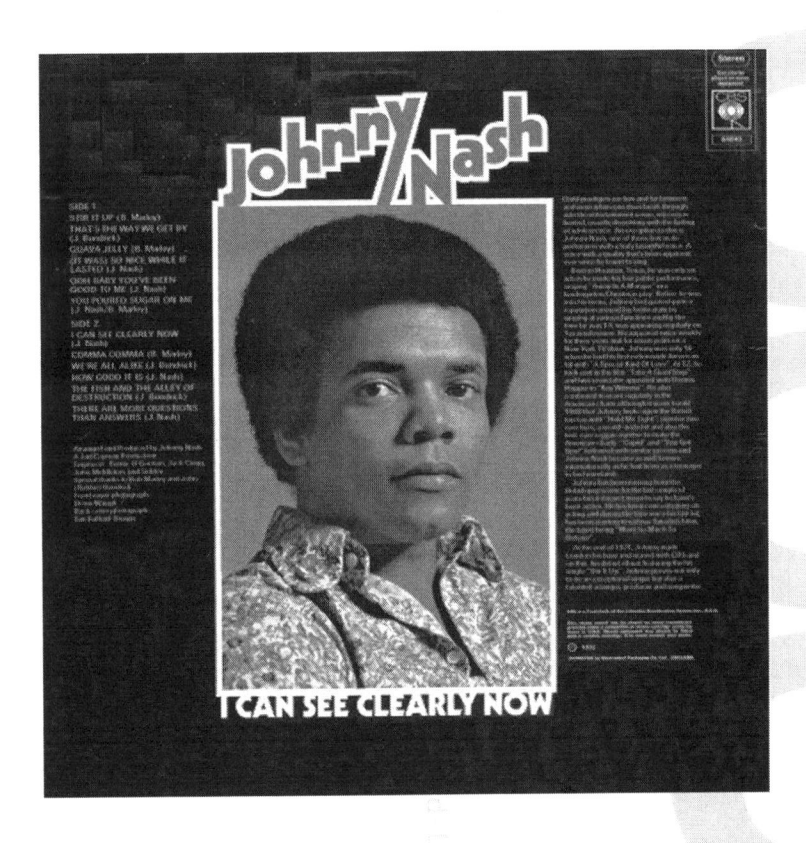

SELECTED SINGLES DISCOGRAPHY 1968 -1972

MAJOR MINOR
MM-586 You Got Soul   1968

REGAL ZONAPHONE
RZ-3010 Hold Me Tight   1968

MAJOR MINOR
MM-603 Cupid   1969
MM-701 (What A) Groovy Feeling   1970

CBS
CBS-7800 Stir It Up   1972
CBS S-8113 I Can See Clearly Now   1972
CBS S-8351 There Are More Questions Than Answers   1972

THE VARIOUS ARTISTS

BORIS GARDNER

Boris Gardner or (Boris Gardiner) was born in Kingston, Jamaica on the 13th January 1943. He spent much of his early years in the music business performing on the hotel circuit during the 1960s. Throughout the emerging years of reggae he worked exclusively as a session musician with The Upsetters, The Aggrovaters and The Chrystallites.

He enjoyed a solo hit in 1970 releasing his own version of 'Elizabethan Serenade' on the Duke label in the UK, DU-39 titled 'Elizabethan Reggae'. The record reached a respectable number 14 in the UK spending over three months on the chart. The record was a popular choice with the skinheads who could dance to the catchy instrumental that would feature on Trojan's first 'Chartbuster' series TBL 105 also released in 1970.

The story goes though that he nearly missed out on the recognition for the single as the label on the original pressings in the UK had credited Byron Lee as the artist, who was the instrumentals record producer. The UK singles chart for the first week on the 17th January and the subsequent re-entry on the 31st and the next four weeks all used Byron Lee as the artist.

However all record and chart data after the 28th February gave Boris Gardner the credit he deserved. Trojan released a debut album the same year 'Reggae Happening' TBL 121. Boris continued to release other material but it only gained success in his native Jamaica until that was almost two decades later in 1986 he when found chart success again with his number one hit, a vocal rendition, 'I Want To Wake Up With You'.

BRUCE RUFFIN

Bruce Ruffin was born Bernardo Constantine Balderamus on the 17th February 1952 in the parish of St. Catherine, Jamaica. He joined The Techniques in 1967 performing as a talented singer and writing material for the group who had enjoyed a string of rocksteady hits in the 1960's. He recorded as a soloist in 1969 'Long About Now'.

The record was a quick tempo reggae track portraying his gentle sweet voice. He continued to release material in the vein of pop-reggae working with the likes of Leslie Kong and Lloyd Charmers releasing a cover versions of Paul Simon's 'Cecilia' but it was another cover version, Jose Feliciano's 'Rain' that gave him a chart hit with Trojan in 1971.

'Rain' was released on Trojan TR-7814 with the B side featuring the popular 'Geronimo', with the record reaching number 19 in May 1971 and featuring on Trojan's extremely popular 'Reggae Chartbusters Volume 3' TBL 169. 1972 saw the release of 'Mad About You' this time on Rhino RNO-101 earning further chart success reaching a commendable number 9 in July.

By this time the unpretentious sound of reggae had moved on, in most cases to a more polished sweetened pop orientated string laden affair, a sound the ebbing ranks of skinheads could no longer empathise with.

TONY TRIBE

A popular choice with the skinheads was 'Red Red Wine' by Tony Tribe with the original release on the Downtown label DT-419 in 1969 having some copies miss credited to Tony Tripe. Despite its popularity and an appearance on top of the pops dressed as a skinhead it only made it to number 46. Another record followed but tragically the singer was killed in a car crash in 1970.

JIMMY LONDON

Jimmy London was born on the 30th November 1949 in the parish of St. Catherine. Jamaica. His early work saw him recording as a member of The Inspirations and spending some time with both Lee 'Scratch' Perry and Joe Gibbs.

His success came when he teamed up with the Impact Allstars at Randy's Studio recording several well received singles including a cover of Simon & Garfunkel's 'Bridge Over Troubled Water' released on Randy's RAN-507 during 1970.

The Trojan subsidiary label was set up to release productions from the late Vincent Chin's Jamaican Randy's and Impact Labels with 'A Little Love' RAN-520 released the following year. Both singles were substantial hits in Jamaica with 'Bridge Over Troubled Water' featuring on Trojan's budget album 'Tighten Up Volume 5'. Both tracks also appeared on his debut album 'Bridge Over Troubled Water' released on Trojan TRLS 39 in 1972.

THE MAYTONES

A Jamaica tradition has always been for a group to form their name from their respective birthplace and The Maytones are no exception. The Maytones who were formed in the late 1960s consisted of Vernon Buckley, Alvin Ranglin and Gladstone Grant.

All three grew up in May Pen in the parish of Clarendon, Jamaica. May Pen having produced several recording artist over the years and perhaps one of its most famous sons has to be Toots Hibbert who formed the Maytals. Much of The Maytones early material was recorded for Alvin Ranglin who had left the group to become their manager.

The first recording session in 1968 saw the subsequent release of 'Billy Goat' a record that was snapped up by Trojan for release in the UK on Blue Cat BS-149.

Trojan launched the GG label in 1970 primarily as an outlet for Alvin Ranglin productions and over its time The Maytones would become the labels most featured artists. The group released several notable singles including their excellent version of Greyhound's 'Black & White' GG-4522 in 1971.

In 1972 the group recorded two versions of 'As Long As You Love Me' GG-4531, a first-rate reggae up beat number with the second a slowed down ballad version. The upbeat recording made it onto Trojan's 'Tighten Up Volume 6' released towards the latter part of 1972.

JACKIE EDWARDS

Wilfred Gerald 'Jackie' Edwards was born in Jamaica in 1940 and spent his teenage years performing covers of American R&B hits. His rich voice was often compared to Nat King Cole and this enabled him to build a solid reputation. Jackie started penning songs when the import of records from America dried up as the focus in America had turned from rhythm & blues to rock & roll, however this led to a demand for more local productions.

The home grown Jamaican R&B was produced primarily for the sound systems of the day with writers blending R&B and calypso and most significantly shifting the accent of the drum from the first and third beats to create ska. Jackie Edwards work was seen as equally influential as the likes of Prince Buster. He worked for Studio One before linking with the up and coming independent producer, Chris Blackwell.

His early Jamaican releases included 'You're Eyes Are Dreaming', 'Tell Me Darling' and 'What's Your Name', the song later used as the inspiration for Boy Friday's 'Version Girl' in 1970. Jackie Edwards immigrated to the UK in the early sixties where he renewed his acquaintance with Chris Blackwell who by now had the beginnings of his business empire, selling singles to specialist shops, often for large amounts of money.

Chris Blackwell identified with Jackie that he had a talent as a writer for Blackwell's groups under his management, one in particular at that time were The Spencer Davis Group. The group had previously had three singles released but they all failed to reach the top 30. They were very much in need of new material and Chris Blackwell asked Jackie to write a song for them, initially as a B side and he penned 'Keep On Running'.

The song earned the group a massive number one hit and remains perhaps their most enduring song. The follow up number one was also penned by Edwards, 'Somebody Help Me Please', a worldwide hit for the group and Chris Blackwell.

Throughout the transition from ska to rocksteady and eventually reggae Jackie Edwards produced some excellent recordings including from 1968 to 1972,' Julie On My Mind' Island WIP-6026, 1968, 'Johnny Gunman' released on Bread BR-1107 and 'In Paradise' Trojan TR-7833 both tracks released during 1971.

Trojan issued an album, 'I Do Love You' TRLS 47 in 1972.

'White Christmas' originally recorded in 1965 was re-released as a single on Trojan TR-7883 in 1972.

Sadly Wilfred 'Jackie' Edwards died in Jamaica on the 9th August 1992, however five years previous to that he had visited the UK to take part in a veterans reggae performance concert in London, an event that he received no money for and paid all his own travelling expenses.

THE ETHIOPIANS

The Ethiopians were formed by Leonard Dillon a native of Port Antonio, Jamaica who was born on the 9th December 1942. Dillon's early influence in the world of music would come from the church before moving to Kingston in 1963.

A chance discussion with Peter Tosh who then introduced Dillon to The Wailers gained him an appointment with Clement 'Coxone' Dodd. The other members of the group were Stephen Taylor and Aston Morris. The group began recording for Dodd as early as 1966.

After Morris, the group songwriter left, The Ethiopians began recording at Dynamic Studios. They later released the time honoured classic hit 'Train To Skaville' issued on the Rio label in 1967, a record that made it to number 40 in the UK chart in September that year.

Further ska classics followed including 'Engine 54' and 'The Whip'. 1968 saw the release of their early reggae hit the critical 'Everything Crash', the track later covered by Prince Buster was released in the UK in 1970 on JJ Records, prefix JJ-3303. The song was criticising the political situation in Jamaica at a time when power and water were being rationed, a move that lead to unrest and in one incident 31 people were shot by the police.

Dillon continued to change producer and between 1969 and 1971 The Ethiopians released material under several producers with singles released on Nu-Beat, Trojan, Bamboo, Duke Reid, GG, Treasure Isle, Big Shot, Explosion and Song Bird. One of the most notable recordings 'Lot Wife' was released on Song Bird SB-1062 in 1971.

The group released two albums both on Trojan, one in 1969 titled 'Reggae Power' TTL 10 and in 1970, 'Woman Capture Man' TBL 112.

ROY SHIRLEY

Roy Shirley was born on the 18th July 1944 in Kingston's Trench Town where he grew up. His early recordings went un-released so he joined Leslie Kong with his first record co-arranged with his close friend Jimmy Cliff. After a spell with Ken Boothe he joined the original Uniques. In 1966 he recorded 'Hold Them' said to be the first record to slow down the infectious ska beat, therefore creating rocksteady. The story goes that the song just would not work with the up tempo ska beat, Joe Gibbs suggested he slowed down the rhythm, a move that created a massive hit in Jamaica.

With no further success following Roy teamed up with Bunny Lee. 1968 saw him set up his own label 'Public' releasing amongst others 'Flying Reggae' and 'Prophecy Fulfilling'. A Jamaican hit came in 1971 with 'A Sugar' a record that was released in the UK in 1972 on both Trojan's Green Door label GD-4026, and on Pama's Punch label PH-108.

DERRICK MORGAN

Derrick Morgan was born on the 27th March 1940 in the parish of Clarendon, Jamaica. At the age of 17 he entered a talent show which he won, receiving a rousing reception. Two years later he began recording for Duke Reid who at the time was resourcing new talent for his Treasure Isle label.

One of Morgan's early records gave him a popular hit in Jamaica 'Fat Man' released on the Blue Beat label, a track that was later re worked in 1970 and issued on the flip side of 'Return Of Jack Slade' released on Pama's Unity label UN-546. During the early years of ska Derrick worked alongside Desmond Dekker, Bob Marley and Jimmy Cliff and it was a meeting with Jimmy Cliff that led to a fruitful relationship with producer Leslie Kong.

Derrick Morgan created a different record in 1960 being the only artist to hold the top seven positions in the Jamaican chart simultaneously. 1961 saw a massive hit for him with the release of 'You Don't Know' a Leslie Kong production later re titled 'Housewife's Choice', now synonymous with the name Derrick Morgan. The record launched a rivalry between him and Prince Buster who accused Derrick of stealing his ideas. Buster released 'Blackhead Chiney Man' taking a swipe at Kong. A counter release was quick to come from Derrick Morgan titled 'Blazing Fire'. Listen to the tracks and you will see how intense the rivalry was.

Other releases and counter releases followed including 'Thirty Pieces Of Silver' from Buster with Morgan responding with 'No Raise No Praise'. Clashes often erupted amongst the respective followers to such an extent the government of the day had to step in. A photo shoot was arranged appearing in the Jamaican Daily Gleaner portraying the rivals as friends.

Derrick Morgan continued to release first class quality material including 'Tougher Than Tough', 'The Conqueror' and 'Seven Letters' cited by some as the first true reggae record, although a fact disputed by others. By this time Island records in the UK had picked up on Derrick's records releasing such tracks as 'Gimme Back' WI-3101 in 1968.

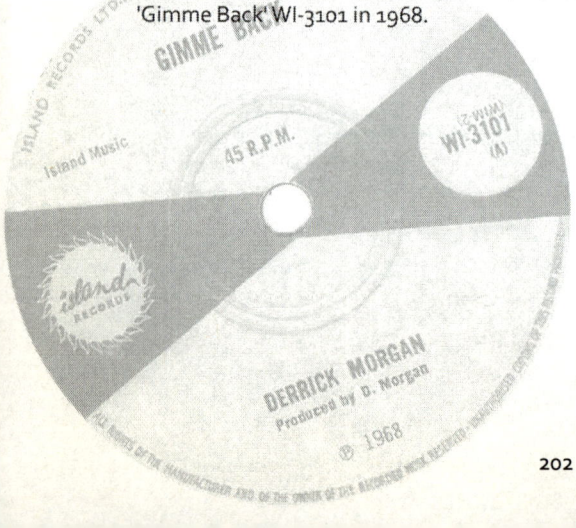

The seeds of an event that had a massive influence on Max Romeo's career were sown in 1968 when Derrick's brother in law Edward 'Bunny' Lee whom Derrick had helped set up in the music industry released Derrick's song 'Hold You Jack' issued in the UK on Island WI-3159. 'Hold You Jack' proved a huge hit for Derrick in Jamaica with the rhythm track used on 'Wet Dream' of which Derrick was scheduled by Bunny Lee to record, One story goes that due to a mix up record salesman Max Romeo stepped in to do the recording and the rest they say on that one is history.

Another track produced by Bunny Lee, 'Seven Letters' was released during 1969 in the UK on the Crab label CRAB-8. With the popularity of reggae in the UK taking off due to the skinheads indulgence Derrick moved to England with Bunny Lee with 1969 seeing their release of the skinhead anthem 'Moon Hop' on Crab CRAB-32 with backing provided by the Rudies.

Bunny 'Striker' Lee born Edward O' Sullivan Lee in 1941 began his music career working as a record plugger, first for Duke Reid then Leslie Kong. The role of the plugger was to visit the record shops with the new releases and plug them with the radio stations to get air play.

His big break came whilst in England when he met the Palmer brothers who gave him an advance to go back to Jamaica and produce some records which he licensed through their Unity label, a subsidiary of Pama.

KEN BOOTHE

Ken Boothe was born in Denham Town, Kingston in 1948. His recording career began as one half of a duo formed with his friend Stranger Cole, releasing recordings under the title Stranger & Ken. Ken's solo career was launched whilst working with Clement 'Coxone' Dodd, releasing several records including the well known single 'The Train Is Coming' backed by The Wailers.

In 1970 Ken switched to Leslie Kong's Beverley's Records and met with immediate success with the launch of 'Freedom Street' released in the UK on Trojan TR-7756 and 'Why Bay Why'. The latter feature on a compilation album titled 'Reggae Party', produced by Leslie Kong and released by courtesy of Trojan Records in the UK on the Music For Pleasure budget album MFP 5176 in 1970.

The tragic untimely death of Leslie Kong in 1971 had far reaching effects on many artists such as Desmond Dekker and Ken Boothe who continued recording for various producers. Ken had to wait a further two years beyond the golden age of reggae for chart success, but when it came it was huge.

His lightened version of reggae would earn the fading Trojan a number 1 hit in the UK with 'Everything I Own'. A sweetened version of the original release was hastily re-launched with the same prefix as the record became popular, aiding its airplay and progress up the chart. The record was unusual as the title 'Everything I Own' was never mentioned on the release as Ken referred to 'Anything I Own'.

The record remained at number 1 for three weeks in 1974 and although it only charted for twelve weeks six of those were in the top 5.

PHYLLIS DILLON

Phyllis Dillon was born in Linstead St. Catherine, Jamaica on the 1st January 1948 and was very much influenced by American singers Connie Francis and Dion Warwick. As has happened with many famous reggae artists Phyllis began here musical career singing at talent shows and it was at one of those competitions that Duke Reid session guitarist Lynn Taitt discovered Phyllis.

At the tender age of 19 she recorded her first single for Duke Reid on Treasure Isle, 'Don't Stay Away' featuring Tommy McCook And The Supersonics. Her original recording of 'It's Rocking Time' would later be used by Alton Ellis as 'Rocksteady'. Another of her popular recordings during the rocksteady era was 'Perfidia'.

From 1967 until 1971 she lead a double life, living in New York but returning to Kingston twice a year to continue recording for Duke Reid. Treasure Isle released an album in 1970 titled 'One Life To Live'.

1971 saw the release of one of her biggest UK successes with the title track 'One Life To Live, One Love To Give' released on Treasure Isle TI-7058 with the track making it onto Trojan's impressive 'Club Reggae Volume 2'. By the time of the release of 'Midnight Confession' on Treasure Isle TI-7070 in 1972 Phyllis had already decided to retire from the recording industry whilst still only 23. In 1998 Phyllis returned to the recording studio to work once again with Lynn Taitt.

The world of reggae lost one of its most enduring talents when Phyllis died of cancer at the age of 56 in 2004.

THE MELODIANS

The band formed in the Greenwich Town area of Kingston in 1965 by Tony Brevett, Brent Dowe and Trevor McNaughton had their first record cut at Coxone Dodd's famous Studio One. The latter part of the rocksteady era saw them release several excellent Jamaican hit singles on Duke Reid's Treasure Isle, most notably, 'You Have Caught Me', 'I'll Get Along Without You', 'You Don't Need Me' and 'A Little Nut Tree' released on Doctor Bird DB-1125 in 1968.

Their biggest commercial success came when they joined forces with Leslie Kong, who was beginning to enjoy unprecedented international success for a Jamaican producer, with the release of 'Sweet Sensation' in 1969. The record was issued in the UK by Trojan TR-695, a record that spent one week in the UK chart In January 1970 and later that year featured on Trojan's first ' Reggae Chartbusters' album.

'Rivers Of Babylon' followed the same year, a massive Jamaican hit and a popular song in the UK released on Summit SUM-8508. Despite failing to chart it enjoyed international success featuring on the outstanding soundtrack of the Jamaican film 'The Harder They Come'.

As with many musicians, The Melodians, did not escape the effect of the untimely death of Leslie Kong in 1971, eventually moving to record with Lee 'Scratch' Perry and Byron Lee.

Their lead singer Brent Dowe released a solo recording in 1971, a cover of Dawn's 'Knock Three Times' that seemed to suit the pop-reggae idiom superbly. The record produced by Leslie Kong was released on Summit SUM-8521 with the track featuring on the superb Trojan 'Club Reggae Volume 2' the same year.

THE ALBUMS

Trojan Records had dominated the UK reggae market since their launch in 1968 to cater for the growing West Indian community and had released over 180 singles on various labels by the dawn of 1969. Traditionally Jamaican music, ska and rocksteady had found success in the singles market with albums seen as a luxury item. Trojan had launched their TRL album series as early as 1968 with just a handful of releases issued by the dawn of 1970. Pama had also released their SECO series featuring the best of their subsidiary labels including Unity, Crab, Nu-Beat, Gas and Bullet.

Trojan helped to revolutionised the album market, launching a budget price series (TTL) in early 1969. Its inaugural release 'Tighten Up' was a compilation of the most popular recent releases, a format that would give wider access to the music. Priced at just 14/6d it was a must have for the skinheads. The budget priced albums had a modest expectation from Trojan but would soon become a winning formula and the 'Tighten Up' series had arrived.

'Reggae Chartbusters' followed with the album that brought the sounds of reggae to the mainstream and made the records that were hitting the charts or just bubbling under the top 50 available through the main high street outlets. Most importantly it enabled the emerging skinheads to own their favourite tunes for a modest outlay of 19/11d.

The first 'Reggae Chartbusters' was released in 1970 and showcased the original tracks that made the breakthrough from the clubs and disco's and brought the sound of reggae to a wider audience, a sound that the skinheads had fully embraced by the summer of 69, starting a love affair that was to last until 1972.

The 'Club Reggae' series launched in 1971 was compiled as the title suggest from singles that were most popular in the clubs, giving a different offering to the chart hits that were outpouring from Trojan at the time, perhaps a more non commercial sound.

The best of the compilation albums now follows with some fantastic collections of early reggae sounds to appreciate, beginning with the original 'Tighten Up' series.

THE HISTORY OF SKINHEAD REGGAE 1968-1972 TIGHTEN UP

tighten up

TIGHTEN UP
KANSAS CITY
SPANISH HARLEM
PLACE IN THE SUN
WIN YOUR LOVE
DONKEY RETURNS
OB-LA-DI, OB-LA-DA
ANGEL OF THE MORNING
FAT MAN
SOUL LIMBO
MIX IT UP
WATCH THIS SOUND

TIGHTEN UP TROJAN RECORDS TTL 1 1969
(Re Issued as TBL 120)

TIGHTEN UP

The opening track would inevitably have to be **'Tighten Up'** the record that gave the series its name. A tune with rocksteady and early reggae influences from the stable of Lee 'Scratch' Perry. The Untouchables would record several tracks for Lee before perusing solo careers as Jimmy London and Billy Dyce. Joya Landis an American based singer had spent time in Kingston and recorded some songs for Duke Reid; one was her inspirational version of **'Kansas City'**.

Lee 'Scratch' Perry forged a long association with Trojan and is here enjoying an outing on track three with a tune that needs no introduction, a fine instrumental release from Val Bennett, **'Spanish Harlem'**.

Another of Lee 'Scratch' Perry's productions feature as track four, a Stevie Wonder number **'A Place In The Sun'** covered by David Isaacs, the song was recorded at Coxsone Dodd's Studio One in Jamaica during 1968. **'Win Your Love For Me'** a Sam Cooke number was produced by Lynford Anderson and was credited to George A Penny. Side one concludes with **'Donkey Returns'** by Brother Dan All Stars, AKA Richard Thompson who was resident in the UK taking influence from Trojan's successful 'Ride Your Donkey' by The Tennors.

Side two gets the proceedings underway with **'Ob-La-De, Ob-La-Da'** a version of The Beatles heavily influenced rocksteady hit penned by Paul McCartney making reference to Desmond Dekker. The reggae version somehow never quite cut it.

Another outing from Joya Landis, a follow up to 'Kansas City' was **'Angel Of The Morning'**, a song that would prove even more popular being a fabulous lilting version of a recording from a US top ten pop hit of the same year. **'Fat Man'** by veteran Derrick Morgan was an updated version of a song he had recorded way back in 1960 as a teenager, a record that was to become one of Jamaica's biggest hits of that year.

It has been well documented that Morgan had cut several tracks for his brother in law Bunny Lee. One being 'Hold You Jack' the forerunner of the rhythm track to be used on Max Romeo's 'Wet Dream' a song that was originally penned for Derrick who had so one story goes refused the opportunity thus giving Max his big break.

Byron Lee And The Dragonaires had begun their career on the hotel circuit. They featured in the James Bond film Dr. No and by the time they had released their own version of Booker T & The MG's **'Soul Limbo'** the group had become steadfastly established. Incidentally the MG's track was to be used for decades by the BBC for their cricket theme tune, ironic given the corporations early reluctance to give airplay to West Indian music.

The Kingstonians would go on to feature on the next two 'Tighten Up' volumes but their first offering in the series **'Mix It Up'** was a sound typical of the time, a fusion of rocksteady and the emerging sounds of reggae. The album came to a close with **'Watch This Sound'** from The Uniques, a famous trio composed of Ken 'Slim' Smith, Lloyd Charmers 'Tyrell' and Martin 'Jimmy' Riley.

The first album of 'Tighten Up' proved to be a successful formula and within a few months a second volume would be launched, the series being the spring board for the future compilation albums in the 'Chartbusters' and 'Club Reggae' series.

The original 'Tighten Up' released during 1969 as TTL 1 appeared on the all orange label. The Album was then re-released as TBL 121 on the perhaps more familiar orange and white label. Volume 2 and 3 were also first issued on TTL later to be re-released on the TBL series.

THE HISTORY OF SKINHEAD REGGAE 1968-1972   TIGHTEN UP

211

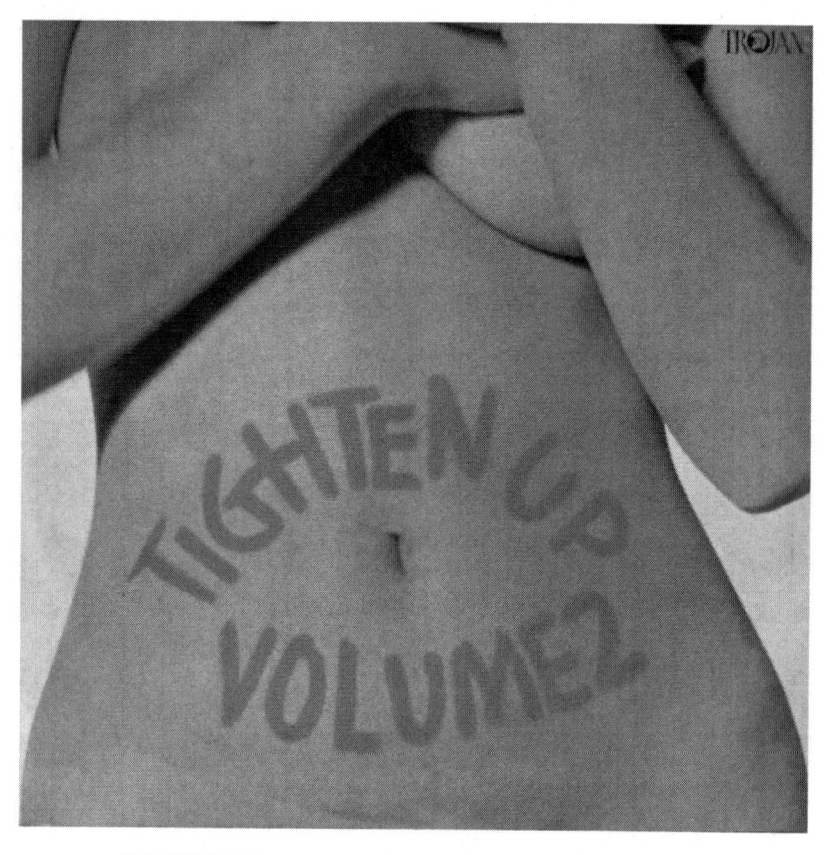

THE HISTORY OF SKINHEAD REGGAE 1968-1972   TIGHTEN UP

TIGHTEN UP VOLUME 2 TROJAN RECORDS TTL 7 1969
(Re Issued as TBL 131)

TIGHTEN UP Volume 2

Probably the best, but almost certainly the most relevant as the second in the series was launched at a time when reggae and the skinheads were truly entwined in a musical love affair. Few would know and how could they that this would be the height of that love affair. The album was a must have for the clean cut cropped headed youth of the day.

The Pioneers had a popular hit with **'Long Shot kick The Bucket'**, one of two chart successes to feature on Volume 2, both as would be expected making it onto the 'Chartbuster' series along with 'Reggae In Your Jeggae'. 'Long Shot kick The Bucket' tells of the demise of Long Shot after 202 races at Kingston's famous Caymanas Park race course.

Rudy Mills **'John Jones'** was a hit in Jamaica quickly released in the UK where it became a firm favourite with the skinheads though never gaining chart success, however that is not what 'Tighten Up' was all about, it was about boss sounds that found favour with the skinheads and their West Indian friends. **'Fire Corner'** from King Stitt, a D.J. who perhaps paved the way for the toaster to make the transition to recording artist and **'Wreck A Buddy'** a risqué outing from The Soul Sisters continues the no nonsense reggae theme.

Dandy's lyrically challenged but none the less highly infectious success comes next **'Reggae In Your Jeggae'** a track released on Thompson's own Downtown label, a subsidiary of Trojan. **'Fattie Fattie'** completes an impressive collection on side one, yet another outstanding offering from Clancy Eccles.

'Return Of Django' from Lee Perry's Upsetters the other chart success to feature on this volume gets side two underway and was Trojan's biggest hit to date reaching number 5 in the British charts.

The Kingstonians feature again this time with **'Sufferer'**, a record that had become a huge hit in Jamaica. They would return again on the forthcoming Volume 3. Joya Landis also featured on the first album in the series and returns with **'Moon Light Lover'**.

'Come Into My Parlour' by the Bleechers was a lively outing as was 'Them A Laugh And A Ki Ki' from The Soul Mates, a group made up of Glen 'Capo' Adams, Alvin Lewis, Max Romeo and George Agard from The Pioneers, who penned the song. An infectious instrumental 'Live Injection' from The Upsetters is track six and concludes the proceedings in a most appropriate fashion on what was the true sound of skinhead reggae.

The tracks on Volume 2 were danceable and energetic and at the budget price distribution of the incessant rhythms was available on the high street for the first time. Reggae was now being sold by one of the major record outlets of the time, Woolworths. Tighten Up Volume 2 proved to be a huge success with the third in the series released in 1970.

TIGHTEN UP VOLUME 3   TROJAN RECORDS   TBL 145   1970

TIGHTEN UP Volume 3

TBL 145 was a reissue of TTL 32 with an altered sleeve.

Trojan had launched the series in 1969 originally on the budget TTL label. Tighten Up TTL 1 showcased the most popular reggae records available in the UK at the time. The decision was taken to continue with the series so here in volume 3.

The Maytals get the proceedings underway with their only UK chart hit **'Monkey Man'** which reached number 47 in May 1970 and needs no introduction. The second offering comes from The Upsetters featuring on vocals Dave Barker, one half of Dave & Ansel Collins. The Upsetters had enjoyed chart success in 1969 with the instrumental 'Return of Django' but **'Shocks Of A Mighty'** is a completely different offering showcasing the vocal talents of Dave Barker that would later come to the fore on 'Double Barrel'.

Ken Boothe's career began way back in the early sixties as part of the duo Stranger & Ken. He later began recording solo with his own inimitable style of soulful vocals displayed here on the Trojan release of **'Freedom Street'**. Ken would go on to achieve cult status with his massive UK number one 'Everything I Own', a recording that would top the charts for three weeks in 1974.

Next up is Dandy Livingstone with **'Raining In My Heart'**. The prolific producer, writer and singer had previously enjoyed success with 'Reggae In Your Jeggae' and 'Rudy A message To You'. Like Ken Boothe he was destined to enjoy further chart success during the early 1970's after the original golden age of reggae had come to an end.

'The Man From Carolina' is next up from the GG Allstars a favourite with the skinheads but failed to chart. Side one concludes with an instrumental **'Leaving Rome'** from Jo Jo Bennett an established Jamaican musician with the rhythm the same as used on the recording 'Rome' a Lloyd Jones song issued on Pama's Bullet BU-429 in 1970.

Side two sees the return of a group having featured on the first two Tighten Up volumes, The Kingstonians this time with **'Singer Man'** a track released on the Song Bird label in 1970. Jimmy Cliff needs no introduction as the singer songwriter later to be actor had already featured on Trojan's 'Reggae Chartbusters' with 'Wonderful World Beautiful People'. **'Suffering In The Land'** would be his penultimate release on Trojan before his move to Island Records where he would enjoy chart success once more with 'Wild World' before his foray into the film industry.

King Stitt was a disc jockey in Kingston and successful singer with his single 'Fire Corner' in 1969 toasting over reggae rhythms. Further success followed for King Stitt, sometimes referred to as the 'Ugly One' with the track featured here **'Herbsman'**.

Songs with innuendoes in the lyrics have always proved popular with Prince Buster and Max Romeo to name but two leading the way. That risqué theme continues here with Nora Dean's **'Barbwire'** a big hit both in the UK and back in Jamaica.

The penultimate offering comes from Delano Stewart who began his career as a member of the Gaylads, although he frequently released solo efforts as here, with **'Stay A Little Bit Longer'**, a song with an up tempo beat. The album concludes with a very popular recording amongst the skinheads, **'Queen Of The World'**, by Lloyd & Claudette, but despite that popularity the record failed to chart.

THE HISTORY OF SKINHEAD REGGAE 1968-1972   TIGHTEN UP

TIGHTEN UP VOLUME 4 TROJAN RECORDS TBL 163 1971

TIGHTEN UP Volume 4

By 1971 reggae had been well and truly accepted into the mainstream although influences were beginning to creep in that would eventually, but not just yet lead to the undoing of its early success. The album opens with the Rastafarian influenced **'Blood And Fire'** from Niney The Observer. Track two needs no introduction and would go on to feature on the soundtrack of the forthcoming film, 'The Harder They Come'. **'Johnny Too Bad'** was released on the Dynamic label by the Slickers, a record drawing attention to the Jamaican Rude Boys who were responsible for violence and crime in their homeland. The legendary group The Ethiopians from the sixties came in with a distinctive sound on **'The Selah'** and feature again on side two with **'Good Ambition'**.

The unmistakable sounds of the Maytals keep the infectious rhythm running with their up tempo **'One Eye Enos'** continuing where they had left off with 'Monkey Man', a track that featured on Volume 3. The next track features Marlene Webber performing well with a heavily accentuated rhythm on her **'Hard Life'**. The first side concludes with Judy Mowatt proclaiming that **'I Shall Sing'**, though sung under the pseudonym of Jean with the backing from the Gaytones. Judy would go onto become a member of Bob Marley's I Three's with fellow vocalist Rita Marley and Marcia Griffiths.

Side two opens with a classic number from Hopeton Lewis showcasing his talented vocal skills as he slows the pace on **'Grooving Out On Life'**. The Pioneers also featured on Tighten Up Volume 2 and continued with their catchy rhythms with **'Starvation'** a track that was highlighting the plight in Africa. **'Bush Doctor'** was an offering from the British based session players, The Music Doctors.

Track four is the second offering from the Ethiopians, a track that continued in their traditional style. Lloydie & The Lowbites became infamous for the risqué album 'Censored' and The Lowbites feature here with **'I Got It'**. 'Censored' was issued through Trojan on the Lowbite label prefix LOW-001 but a second album volume 2 although planned was never issued. Pama had released an earlier album of ribald but infectious skinhead reggae material titled 'Birth Control' on Pama SECO 32 in 1970, the title track utilised by The Specials for their number one hit 'Too Much Too Young' a decade later. **'Stand By Your Man'**, brought about a total change of style and concluded yet another exceptional collection of reggae, from Marlene Webber with her resounding version of a famous Tammy Wynett number.

THE HISTORY OF SKINHEAD REGGAE 1968-1972   TIGHTEN UP

TIGHTEN UP   VOLUME 5   TROJAN RECORDS   TBL 165   1971

TIGHTEN UP volume 5

Number five in the series came some three years after the inaugural release, the series having gone from strength to strength, although perhaps not known at the time this would be the last truly authentic offering in the series.

The opening track featured Delroy Wilson with his classic, **'Better Must Come'**. Delroy had started out at Coxone Dodd's Studio One and was now somewhat of a veteran on the reggae circuit at the young age of 22. The track was released on the Jackpot label JP-763 in 1971.

Track two **'In Paradise'** is a soulful ballad in Jackie's imitable style and was released on Trojan TR-7833, a duo with Judy Mowatt, although credited on the label as Julie Anne. Next up is a change of pace from Clancy Eccles prodigies The Dynamites with their own rendition of **'Hullo Mother'**, a somewhat interesting instrumental. Clancy himself is up next with **'Rod Of Correction'**, a distinctive Clancy rhythm with his characteristic vocals enduring throughout.

Dennis Alcapone comes in with his talk-over version of his fellow studio artist Eric Donaldson's rendition of 'Cherry Oh Baby'. Dennis' distinctive vocals are showcased here on **'Ripe Cherry'**, the same combination was used on his famous 'Guns Don't Argue' utilising Eric's 'Love Of The Common People'. A medley concludes side one from Errol Dunkley aptly titled **'Three In One'** a collection of old hits released on Big BG-327, with the B side titled 'One In Three'.

Side two gets under way with a record that suited the 'pop reggae' idiom **'Joy To The World'** from Julien And The Chosen Few, actually Julie Anne who as we have already discovered on the album is in fact Judy Mowatt, the record produced by Sonia Pottinger was released on High Note HS-054.

Next up is **'Know For I'** a track from Bong Herman and Bunny, who as the sleeve notes mentioned sound very much like the Ethiopians on this infectious medium tempo number. No mistaking who is up next on track three, it's of course The Maytals with their **'It's You'**, slightly slower than their normal pace but still maintaining an intense feel.

The pace changes again with track four from Jimmy London with his rendition of the Simon & Garfunkel classic **'Bridge Over Troubled Waters'** released on Randy's RN-507 in 1970, incidentally the inspiration for an album of the same name during 1972.

The penultimate is another well know cover, this time **'Shaft'** from the Chosen Few, the well known theme tune from the popular film of the day. The album concludes with a record already well documented in the book **'Duppy Conqueror'** from Bob Marley And The Wailers.

There were reputed to have been three different pressing of Tighten Up Volume 5 TBL 165. The pressing listed here but also one with Peter Tosh's 'Memphis' in place of 'Duppy Conqueror' and another with 'Know For I' featuring twice.

TIGHTEN UP VOLUME 6 TROJAN RECORDS TBL 185 1972

TIGHTEN UP Volume 6

Although not the last in the series, volume 6 would be the last that held true to the previous offerings at a time when reggae was rapidly declining in favour with the skinheads, who had four years earlier helped elevate reggae to the world stage. However sweetening many of the releases with sophisticate string arrangements would prove costly for Trojan at a time when the traditional skinhead movement was also in decline.

The collection here although not quite on par with previous offering in the 'Tighten Up' series does contain a few gems. The Maytones maintain an incessant rhythm on **'As Long As You Love Me'**, released on the GG label in 1972. The Maytones as we had discovered were formed in the late sixties and comprised Vernon Buckley and Gladstone Grant, both of whom lived in May Pen, Clarendon, Jamaica, which had inspired the group's name.

Harry J Allstars **'Down Side Up'** was another notable offering from the talented producer, Harry Johnson and was released in 1972 on the Harry J label. Side one ends with a chartbuster, a rare outing for Tighten Up from Dandy AKA Robert Thompson to name just one. **'Suzanne Beware Of The Devil'** was a big hit for Dandy Livingstone one of the last as the golden age of reggae was drawing to a close, the only others to make the top 30 would be Johnny Nash 'There Are More Questions Than Answers' and Judge Dread with 'Big Seven' ironically using the same rhythm track featuring on **'President Mash Up The Resident'** a good offering on the album from Shortie.

Side two kicked off with a cover version of Jimmy Cliff's **'Struggling Man'** by the British based group the Cimarons, who performed admirably with a good up tempo version, although very pop influenced. Next The Maytals with **'Redemption Song'** another excellent offering from the legendary group.

The penultimate track came from the soulful Jackie Edwards, 'Who Told You So'. The album closes with a reverberating sound from Clancy Eccles in his usual upbeat quality vein with the rousing, **'Unite Tonight'**.

The Tighten Up series continued with another two volumes 7 and 8 acting as an outlet for Trojan's continued production into 1973. A further album was scheduled, Tighten Up volume 9 TBL 211 but was never issued.

No comprehensive sleeve notes on volume 6

REGGAE CHARTBUSTERS   TROJAN RECORDS TBL 105   1970

REGGAE CHARTBUSTERS

The album gets underway with **'Wonderful World Beautiful People'** by Jimmy Cliff released in 1969 peaking in the chart at number 6, one of three chart successes for Jimmy over the next year or so. Track two is a record by producer Dandy, **'Reggae In Your Jeggae'** although it never made the British charts it was a popular choice with the skinheads. Next up was **'Israelites'** released on Pyramid in 1968 a record seen by most as the defining influence for reggae. On its release it had little airplay but became popular with the skinheads who heard it in the clubs and disco's. It started to receive air play in early 1969 presenting a total new sound to those not familiar with Jamaican music. 'Israelites' entered the charts in March 1969 and by mid April was sitting proudly at the top of the pile, the first reggae number one in the UK.

The skinheads who embraced reggae from its evolvement from rocksteady in 1968 had a tribute paid to them with the next track **'Skinhead Moonstomp'**. The moonstomp theme no doubt influenced from the events of July 1969, and man's first landing on the moon. It was a foot stomping offering from Symarip popular of course with the skinheads but never breaking into the top 50. The famous album followed with a host of bracer snapping tracks suited to the skinhead theme. The penultimate track on side one sees The Pioneers **'Poor Rameses'** a record released after their massive hit 'Long Shot Kick The Bucket' that features on side two.

Side one concludes with an instrumental that became an anthem for the skinheads, **'Liquidator'** by Harry J Allstars, a Harry J production, who also had his own record label back in Jamaica, released in the UK through Trojan on the Harry J label in 1969. 'Liquidator' peaked at number 9 in November 1969 and spent some twenty weeks on the chart. November 1969 was a month that saw three reggae records in the top 10 and a further two within the top 50.

'Liquidator' was adopted as an anthem played before matches by some football clubs but was dropped as it was said to have encourage violence amongst rival skinheads. 1970 was a truly heady time of chart success for Trojan and reggae in general.

Side two opens with another instrumental this time by The Upsetters **'Return Of Django'** released on Trojan's Upsetter label in 1969 and the title track from the LP TRL 19 released by Trojan in 1970, again on the Upsetter label. Composed by Lee 'Scratch' Perry in the true vein of pure reggae it spent a respectable three weeks at number 5 in November 1969.

Another popular choice for the skinheads was **'Red, Red, Wine'** by Tony Tribe featured on track two with the original release on the Downtown label DT-419 in 1969 with some copies miss credited to Tony Tripe. Despite its popularity and an appearance on top of the pops dressed as a skinhead it only made it to number 46. Another record followed but tragically the singer was killed in a car crash in 1970.

Third up needs no introduction, the 1969 release by The Pioneers telling the tale of **'Long Shot Kick The Bucket'** recorded for Beverley's, the record had a true Jamaican feel to it. The record received little air play on its release but by the autumn of 69 it was added to the BBC's play list reaching number 21 in November, and remaining on the chart for a total of eleven weeks. Track four features another instrumental, **'Elizabethan Reggae'** again finding popularity with the skinheads it was released on Trojan's Duke label and made it to number 14 in March 1970. The record was the only chart success for Boris Gardner of the era but he was to achieve a number one spot with a vocal offering almost two decades later.

Next comes **'It Miek'** sometimes spelt 'It Mek' released in 1969 as a follow up to Desmond Dekker's massive hit 'Israelites', a record incidentally that was still on the charts when 'It Mek' was climbing to give Desmond a hat-trick of chart success where it would spend two weeks at number 7 in July of that year. **'Sweet Sensation'** was a record that managed just one week on the chart at number 41 in January 1970 and completes the line up of a dozen chartbusters. A first rate offering from The Melodians being a fast moving melodic reggae number in a similar vein to many tracks that would feature on the forthcoming 'Reggae Chartbusters volume 2'. The Melodians would go onto record their biggest success 'Rivers Of Babylon' a song that would feature on the soundtrack of the forthcoming Jamaican film 'The Harder They Come'.

REGGAE CHARTBUSTERS VOLUME 2
TROJAN RECORDS TBL 147   1970

REGGAE CHARTBUSTERS Volume 2

Following on from the highly successful 'Reggae Chartbusters ' a second volume was issued in 1970 on Trojan's budget TBL series priced at 19/11, or as we would say today 98 pence. The series proved popular as it allowed the emerging skinheads to get hold of all their favourite reggae records as many would not be able to afford the scores of singles that were being released at this time, remembering volume one was only issued in April of the same year.

It was obvious by now that reggae was not to be the flash in the pan that several commentators of the time were predicting. Reggae had moved on a pace from the original releases on volume one as that album covered records released in 1969 through to 1970.

The 'Chartbusters' albums should not be underestimated in their promotion of reggae as for the first time reggae was being sold in the mainstream outlets, and was now being heard outside of the school disco and the clubs for the first time.

As the hits continued to come reggae began to receive far more airplay at the BBC and began to lose the stigma of being crude and basic, with this volume highlighting the melodic harmonies and strings of the evolving music. Not perhaps as authentic as the original sounds of 1968 but nevertheless reggae was now appealing to the masses and enjoying a period of unprecedented success.

The first track needed no introduction, nor the artist, it had reached a respectful number 2 in the charts, in fact a first chart hit for Desmond Dekker since parting from The Aces. Desmond had previously enjoyed chart success with The Aces in 1970 with 'Pickney Gal' also featured on this album and prior to that in 1967 '007' and 'Israelites' and 'It Miek' in 1969. **'You Can Get It If You Really Want'** was a huge hit for Desmond, a song penned by Jimmy Cliff, one that would go on to feature on the soundtrack of 'The Harder They Come' albeit Jimmy Cliff's original version. Following his previous chart success Desmond had by now moved to England where he would remain.

Second up is Freddie Notes And The Rudies with **'Montego Bay'** just charting at number 45, being a cover version of Bobby Bloom's that enjoyed considerable chart success at the same time. The song tells of life in Montego Bay with the opening line telling that Vernon'll meet him when his Boeing lands and letting him know that the keys to his MG will be waiting in his hand.

Track three, a record that would launch Nicky Thomas to a worldwide audience with **'Love of The Common People'** was a very melodic song that peaked at number 9 enjoying fourteen weeks on the charts earlier in 1970. Following the records success Nicky moved to England. It was however to be Nicky's only chart success but as has been said before good records do not always achieve charts recognition and Nicky continued to produce and record several excellent tracks before his untimely death in 1990.

Fourth up was **'What Greater Love'** by Teddy Brown who only released a few singles, this being his most popular with a follow up 'Rose Garden', tracks that were very pop-reggae influenced and very melodic. Teddy's voice was used on many records to help sweeten the sound.

Next comes **'Pickney Gal'** a hit for Desmond Dekker And The Aces earlier in the year, the last of Desmond's recordings with the Aces reaching number 42 in January 1970, before going solo with the release of 'You Can Get It If You Really Want'.

The last track of side one was **'Message From A Blackman'** by Derrick Harriott who had enjoyed a good number of releases during the ska and rocksteady years. 'Message From A Blackman' was released on the Song Bird label in 1970, an offering that was somewhat different than the rest of the tracks on this album, delivering as the title suggests a message with a somewhat surreal feel to the record. Although selling well it never entered the British chart.

Side two kicks off again with a record that requires no introduction and very little explanation, it is **'Young Gifted And Black'** by Bob &Marcia. Bob is of course Bob Andy and Marcia is Marcia Griffiths both individual performers in their own right. The record was released on Trojan's Harry J label with strings added to the original Jamaican version, reaching a respectable number 5 and spending a creditable twelve weeks on the chart.

Track two, **'Monkey Man'** by Toots And The Maytals, was a Leslie Kong produced record although it is said that Toots was having a dig at Leslie Kong. Surprisingly the record only achieved a number 47 in the UK and was the only British chart success for Toots and The Maytals. Now that old saying about not getting into the chart certainly runs true for The Maytals who were one of the most popular and prolific reggae groups with their own distinctive style.

Next up is a complete change of style with a track from Horace Faith, **'Black Pearl'**, a record that was to some extent over cooked and a far cry for the pure reggae that endeared the skinheads, amongst others. However it did sell well and gained the only hit for Horace reaching number 13. It was described at the time as 'swamped with pop hooks' nevertheless it was a huge hit spending some ten weeks on the chart.

Nicky Thomas features again with his follow up to 'Love Of The Common People', an extremely hard act to follow and he never enjoyed its success with **'God Bless The Children'**. The record lacked the same melodic commercial appeal and failed to make the chart.

The penultimate offering, the second on the compilation from The Rudies was **'Patches'** a cover of a huge hit for Clarence Carter. A cover version of a pop hit in reggae was often released and did sometimes work, on this occasion it worked extremely well, despite this the record failed to provide a second chart success for The Rudies who would soon reform as Greyhound.

The album ends with Jimmy Cliff's rendering of **'Vietnam'**, a hard-hitting account of the troubles of the time. Surprisingly this was only Jimmy's second chart hit but not gaining the heady heights of his first, reaching only number 46, and charting for just three weeks. That completed the line up of 'Chartbusters' but reggae was still at its height and more chart success would follow.

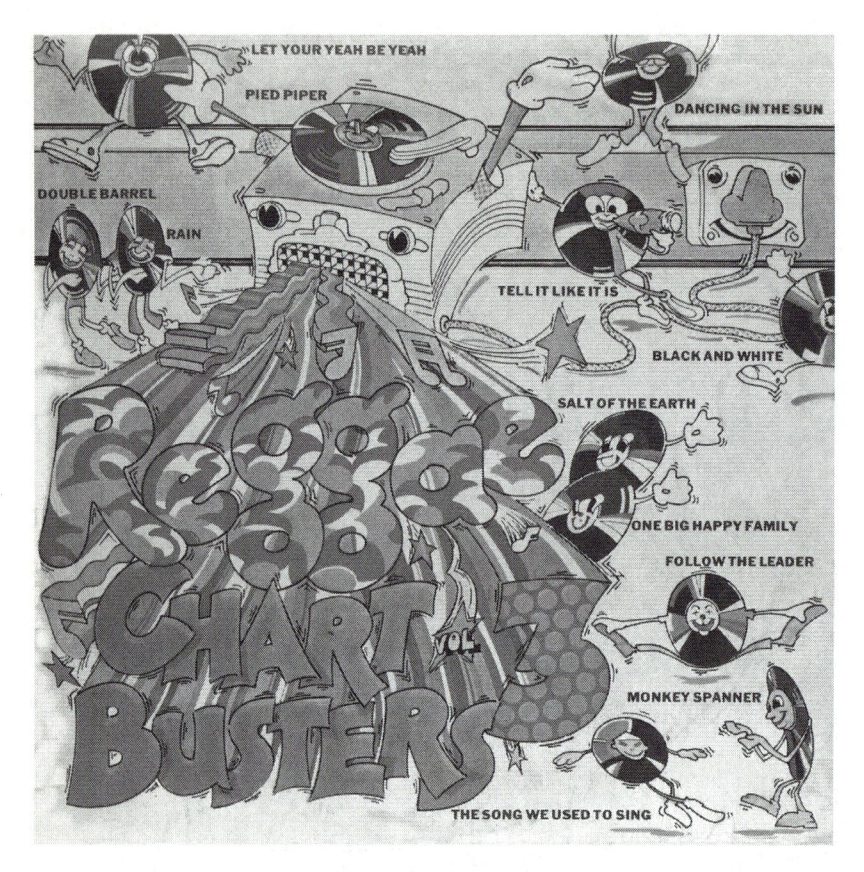

THE HISTORY OF SKINHEAD REGGAE 1968-1972   REGGAE CHARTBUSTERS

REGGAE CHARTBUSTERS VOLUME 3
TROJAN RECORDS TBL 169 1971

REGGAE CHARTBUSTERS Volume 3

The third in the series of 'Reggae Chartbusters' continued the theme with the records that had entered the charts or flirted just outside. The difference in the style of reggae from that first volume is very evident here with the album kicking off with The Pioneers Jimmy Cliff penned song, **'Let Your Yeah Be Yeah'**.

A while had passed since The Pioneers previous chart success with 'Long Shot Kick The Bucket' back in 1969. This was a change in direction for The Pioneers who had several excellent releases since that hit including 'Black Bud' and 'Samfie Man', but chart success had eluded them. Now offering a more pop driven, string laden sound that was to bring them a top 5 hit in September 1971, spending twelve weeks on the chart.

Track two sees Nicky Thomas back following his 'Love Of The Common People' with a somewhat different offering of an Aaron Neville tune but despite good sales it failed to make the charts. **'Tell It Like It Is'** was the A side with the B side 'BBC' having a dig at the reluctance of the nations radio station to give reggae the airplay it deserved.

Track three was the second of the massive chart success for Dave & Ansel Collins with **'Monkey Spanner'**. A refreshing change for the purists of raw reggae, released on the Techniques label it was a true unpretentious sounding track with the opening line declaring that 'This is a heavy heavy monster sound'. 'Monkey Spanner' spent three weeks at number 7 in July 1971 not quite reaching the height of it forerunner earlier in the year.

Greyhound continue the hits on track four with **'Follow The Leader'** but alas did not follow on the success achieved with 'Black and White'. The record lacking the brilliance of that previous offering but they would enjoy renewed chart success later with their rendition of 'Moon River' a track that would have almost certainly featured if there had been a follow up album 'Chartbusters Volume 4'.

Track five sees another outing for Bob And Marcia following on from their previous hit 'Young Gifted And Black' this time out with **'Pied Piper'** continuing in the same melodic vein but with a change of content from their previous outing. As with several of their compatriots the follow up did not emulate the previous offering but 'Pied Piper' did achieve a respectable number 11 in July 1971, a month that saw three reggae records in the top 30.

Side one is concluded with **'One Big Happy Family'** by Bruce Ruffin a track fully aimed at the pop-reggae market, although it failed to achieve the same impact as his previous hit 'Rain' with chart entry eluding him this time.

Side two begins with a number one, we have already heard about 'Monkey Spanner' but earlier in 71 **'Double Barrel'** was to introduce Dave & Ansel Collins, incidentally the duo who were assumed by many to be brothers were in fact Dave Barker and Ansel Collins. 'Double Barrel' was a huge hit in Jamaica. Released in the UK on Trojan's Techniques label it was initially given little airplay but was soon to storm the charts entering at 43 in March 1971, by now receiving good coverage on radio. It reached the heady heights of number 1 in May where it remained for two weeks, spending seven weeks in the top 10 and a total of fifteen weeks on the chart.

Track two performed by Daniel In The Lion's Den AKA The Rudies, **'Dancing In The Sun'** continues the pop-reggae vein, a catchy tune featuring Carl Douglas who later found fame with 'Kung Fu Fighting'. Moving onto track three we find Greyhound again with a track that we have already mentioned.

It seems that the tracks for 'Chartbusters' were not in chronological order but were set out to provide a good overall variety of reggae and it worked. **'Black And White'** was Greyhound first outing having reformed from The Rudies and was to be the first of three chart successes they would enjoy, the others mentioned previously were 'Moon River' and later in 1972 they would come again with 'I am What I Am', a certainty for that elusive volume 4.

Dandy is next up with **'Salt Of The Earth'**, Dandy would have to wait until the summer of 1972 before enjoying chart success with 'Suzanne Beware Of The Devil' as this bouncy number, a cover of a Jagger Richardson song failed to chart. Track eleven is another from Bruce Ruffin 'Rain' released before his previous offering on the album and unlike 'One Big Happy Family' it did enter the charts peaking at number 19 during May of 1971 spending eleven weeks on the chart. Bruce had moved to London to continue his career after the success of **'Rain'**.

Desmond Dekker concludes side two with **'The Song We Used To Sing'** a catchy number, being the follow up on Trojan to Desmond's smash hit 'You Can Get It If You Really Want'. The track was perhaps over produced moving away from the raw sound of Desmond's earlier patois influenced hits and the free flowing excellent 'You Can Get It If You Really Want'. It failed to give Desmond another run at the chart.

With 1971 drawing to a close the previous chart success would never be emulated with only a handful of chart entries to follow before the end of 1972, Trojan never released a 'Chartbusters Volume 4', but did continue to produce a few good records that featured on 'Tighten Up' and 'Club Reggae' through the remainder of 1972.

CLUB REGGAE   TROJAN RECORDS TBL 159   1971

CLUB REGGAE

The first in Trojan's successful Club Reggae series was launched on the TBL prefix and would soon be followed by Volume 2 the same year. Jamaican music did not fall well into the album market until Trojan came up with the idea of the budget priced albums using singles that had so called peaked in sales then compiling them onto budget priced LP's. The idea would prove to be very successful as it enabled many of the working class youths, who in most cases could not get hold of the many singles that were being released in ever increasing numbers, to own their favourite tunes.

The 'Club Reggae' series was compiled as the title suggest from singles that were most popular in the clubs giving a diverse offering to the chart hits that were outpouring from Trojan at the time, although some tracks crossed over most notably here with Dave And Ansel Collins number one chart hit 'Double Barrel'.

The Club reggae series was said to have run a close second to the most popular Tighten Up compilations, certainly the first three in the series would contain some excellent sounds. The Club Reggae idea was not though new as Island had previously issued Club Ska and Club Rocksteady compilation albums.

Side one gets underway with **'Holly Holy'** from the Fabulous Flames, a record written by Neil Diamond and produced by Clancy Eccles first released on Clandisc CLA-224 in 1970 and featuring Lord Creator's 'Kingston Town' on the B side.

Track two however requires no introduction, **'54-46 Was My Number'** an updated reggae version of the groups rocksteady hit from 1968, '54-46 That's My Number', this track issued on Trojan TR-7808 with a version on the flip side by Beverley's Allstars. Both tracks were produced by the legendary Leslie Kong who sadly passed away the same year. Track three is the chart topping hit from early 1970 by Dave And Ansel Collins, **'Double Barrel'** the second release on the new Techniques label TE-901.

The tempo then slows with Derrick Harriott's **'Groovy Situation'** released on the Song Bird label SB-1042. The perpetual Dandy is up next with **'Take A Letter Maria'** this time released under his own name, a track issued on Trojan TR-7800 in 1970.

Side one concludes with an emerging talk over song **'Wear You To The Ball'** by Hugh Roy & John Holt, a track produced by Duke Reid and released on Duke Reid DR-2513 again in 1970, the song being a reworking of The Paragons Jamaican rocksteady hit of the same name for whom John Holt was a member.

Side two gets underway with a record that would feature on the soundtrack of the forthcoming blockbuster Jamaican film 'The Harder They Come', **'Rivers Of Babylon'** from The Melodians, another track produced by Leslie Kong and released on Summit SUM-8508 in 1970. 'Rivers Of Babylon' continued the theme of including records that had peaked in terms of sales but were still very much a part of the current sounds of the day.

Track two is a complete change of pace with an offering from Andy Capp **'The Law'**, a Byron Lee production issued on Duke DU-69 again being a release from the previous year. **'Hitching A Ride'** by A.L.T. Joe AKA Trevor Aljoe was a cover version of a hit for Vanity Fair from 1969.

The Pioneers were up next with **'I Need Your Sweet Inspiration'** a more commercial sound than they had previously found chart success with the track being released on Trojan TR-7795 in 1970.

The penultimate track features an up tempo instrumental from Selwyn Baptiste of Freddie Notes And The Rudies 'Montego Bay' complete with accompanying steel drum on **'Mo' Bay'**.

The first volume of Club Reggae signs off with another upbeat sound this time from Hopeton Lewis with an admirable delivery of **'Boom-Shacka-Lacka'**, an excellent Duke Reid production issued on Duke Reid DR-2505 released in 1970.

Soon to follow hot on the trail of 'Club Reggae' would be one of the most exciting compilation albums that Trojan would release; 'Club Reggae Volume 2' was issued a few months later the same year.

Cherry Oh Baby
Eric Donaldson

Little Boy Blue
Verne and Son

To The Fields
Herman

Sweet Jamaica
Clancy Eccles

It's Too Late
Laurel Aitken

**One Life To Live,
One Love To Give**
Phillis Dillon

Knock Three Times
Brent Dowe

Can't Hide The Feeling
The Gaylads

My Sweet Lord
Byron Lee and
The Dragonaires

Version Girl
Boy Friday

Small Axe
Bob Marley and The Wailers

I Love Jamaica
Neville

CLUB REGGAE VOLUME 2 TROJAN RECORDS TBL 164 1971

CLUB REGGAE Volume 2

1971 witnessed the release of the second in the 'Club Reggae' series and an album of great diversification with every track a true masterpiece of Jamaican music. Following on from the successful launch of what was seen as the best reggae album released in 1971, 'Club Reggae', this compilation came with a truly comprehensive set of sleeve notes from Rob Bell, so good that here they are in full.

One of the best reggae albums released in 1971 was 'Club Reggae' (TBL 159) which featured those records most popular in the discotheques. Such a successful compilation had to be followed by a second volume, so voila.

Kicking off side one is twenty three year old Eric Donaldson singing his big hit of the year **'Cherry Oh Baby'** amid stiff competition, the song won the 1971 Jamaican Festival Song, gaining a festival Gold Medal, the Desno and Geddes award and a cash prize for Eric. Quite a feature for his first recording! The song has a hypnotic bass-dominated rhythm and features Eric's acrobatic voice feeling the way around the lyric. **'Little Boy Blue'** is uncompromising reggae with a tight yet swinging guitar and organ.

Verne and Son sound in fine fettle on this song; their first recording I believe. Produced by A. Ranglin of G.G. Records, who has been responsible for such past hits as 'African Melody' and 'Man From Carolina'.

There was a time when instrumental reggae was the order of the day, and, although now it is usually the vocal records which are more popular, the occasional instrumental is still a force to be reckoned with, for instance **'To The Fields'** by Herman From the opening insinuating words from Herman to the closing bars, the number really moves. Herman is in fact Herman Chin-Loy, owner of Aquarius Records and also co-producer of Bruce Ruffin's recent hit 'Rain'.

Organ and piano lead the intro for Clancy Eccles' **'Sweet Jamaica'** and indeed the organist holds the rhythm together all the way through the number, employing the 'creeping' technique which proved so popular on Clancy's production of 'Holly Holy'. Clancy is of course, one of the veterans of the Jamaican entertainment scene, and is also an accomplished song writer 'Sweet Jamaica' being one of his own compositions.

Laurel Aitken is another pioneer of West Indian music, and was indeed one of the first Jamaican artists to settle in the U.K. **'It's Too Late'**, his own composition, is somewhat reminiscent of the style of the Drifter's records of the early sixties, although completely stamped with Laurel's own personality. Laurel also produced the number himself, an activity which is taking up more and more of his time these days.

Jamaica has produced some great female singers, from Patsy and Millie to Cynthia Richards, Marcia Griffiths and the greatly underrated Phillis Dillon. Phillis has been recording for quite some time, but up to the time she teamed with top producer Duke Reid, she had not met with the success she really deserved. **'One Life To Live, One Love To Give'** was the turning point, and reached the Top Ten in Jamaica. She possesses a most distinctive voice which seems to float from note to note with her seemingly effortless ease on this number, a perfect foil for her accompanying group.

Every now and then a pop number turns up which is ideally suited to the reggae idiom, and the mammoth pop hit of 1971 **'knock Three Times'** falls neatly into that category. Brent Dowe, lead singer with the Melodians made his first solo recording with the Dawn number, and scored immediately. The record was produced by Leslie Kong of Beverleys records, who so sadly passed away in the summer of 1971.

Former label mates of Brent Dowe and the Melodians were the Gaylads who hit the Jamaican charts with **'Can't Hide The Feeling'**, and it is possibly the best record they have ever made, with a great vocal arrangement and a superb production. One to play to those people who still put down Jamaican music as being crude and monotone.

Byron Lee and the Dragonaires have been the top band in the Caribbean for nearly ten years now and are now on the verge of achieving international acclaim. They have toured America, the UK, Canada and many other countries, and everywhere they go, the most requested item is their version of George Harrisons' **'My Sweet Lord'**, featuring band vocalist Keith Lynn. Keith, although fairly diminutive in size, is very much a giant in terms of vocal stature as any follower of the twelve piece band will testify.

The last year has seen the emergence of the 'Version' either being the instrumental of a vocal, or a record brought 'up to date' by dubbing the voice of a D.J. over the old tape. Examples of the latter are any U-Roy or Dennis Alcapone records, both noted for their fast talking rhymes using local slang and dialect, and thus quite often making the words completely unintelligible to an English audience. Producer Dandy gently satirizes the situation with his **'Version Girl'** sung by Boy Friday, a relatively unknown singer whose voice sounds suspiciously familiar!

One of the longest established vocal groups from Jamaica are the Wailers who were hitting he high spots back in the early sixties with such titles as 'Hooligan' 'What's New Pussycat' and many more. The two lead singers are Peter Touch and Bob Marley, although it seems to be Bob Marley who now takes the leading role. They have hit the Jamaican charts several times this year, the biggest success being 'Duppy Conquer' and **'Small Axe'**. 'Small Axe' is a superb example of their fine harmonizing and Bob Marley's controversial lyrics.

The last few months have seen a rash of songs praising Jamaica – Clancy Eccles 'Sweet Jamaica', Honey Boy's 'Jamaica', Greyhound's 'Funky Jamaica' and Neville's 'I Love Jamaica'. Neville wrote, sung and produced **'I Love Jamaica'** for Ken Khouri's Federal Records, and what a success it has been! It is a strange record-predominantly a reggae although the vocal is very much calypso influenced. Nevertheless- a fine record, as indeed is the whole album. I hope you enjoy it as much as we enjoyed putting it together.
Rob Bell.

These sleeve notes on 'Club Reggae Volume 2' are the most comprehensive issued on the Trojan TBL label at a time when an LP cost just 19/11. Looking back now it is pleasing to see that Rob Bell had an eye for talent when recognising the remarkable Bob Marley before he became famous on the World stage admirably supported by the great Peter Tosh or as noted on the sleeve Peter Touch.

The budget priced Club Reggae TBL series continued only out sold by the most famous of Trojan's collections Tighten Up with 'Club Reggae Volume 3' being released in 1972. A further album was issued late 1972 'Club Reggae Volume 4' but by this time the pop infused reggae produced in the UK was very different from those early sounds emanating from Jamaica.

CLUB REGGAE VOLUME 3   TROJAN RECORDS TBL 178   1972

CLUB REGGAE Volume 3

I can recall that the release of 'Club Reggae Volume 3' was eagerly awaited and even the BBC had made reference to its release. It was not to disappointment with the album art work looking superb. Opening the proceedings was Dennis Alcapone with his scorching **'Alcapone's Guns Don't Bark'**. Dennis Alcapone was one of the original DJ's, a gifted performer with amazing talent. Influenced by U Roy, his excellent DJ skills are to the fore here as he toasts over Eric Donaldson's 'Love of the Common People'.

After featuring on Trojan's 'Reggae Chartbuster' following huge success in the British charts with hits such as 'Wonderful World Beautiful People' Jimmy Cliff makes his debut on the 'Club Reggae' compilation with a rather different outing **'Those Good, Good Old Days'**. Next up were The Uniques with a rather vivacious version of Paul Simon's **'Mother And Child Reunion'**, a record that was riding high for Paul Simon in the UK charts peaking at number 5 in March 1972. Paul Simon, one half of the famous duo Simon & Garfunkle had travelled to Jamaica to record the track at Dynamic Studios to capture an authentic Jamaican sound.

Desmond Dekker's first contribution to the 'Club Reggae' series **'Live And Learn'** was a medley of his previous hits including 'Sabotage'. King Iwah and the Upsetters **'Give Me Power'** and the Deltons instrumental **'Chopsticks'** concluded side one of the album.

Side two continued in the same vein as side one with tracks from God Sons **'Merry Up'**, Rocking Horse **'Hard Time'** and Soul Syndicate with **'Riot'** all continuing the sound of the clubs, a sound that would have received very little if any air play from the BBC.

The Fabulous Five are up next with a brilliant up tempo track **'Come Back And Stay'**. The group had only formed in 1970, this being their first single, a record incidentally that made it to number one in Jamaica. The Fabulous Five provided the backing for Johnny Nash on his album 'I Can See Clearly Now', an album that inevitably helped to establish Bob Marley as a major international songwriter following the success of 'Stir It Up' and 'Guava Jelly'.

The penultimate track, **'Just A Dream'**, came from Slim Smith who was one of the most soulful and accomplished singers of rocksteady, and reggae. He performed solo as well as being a member of The Techniques also performing with The Gaylads before joining The Uniques. Many different stories surround the death of Slim in 1973 but what is certain that his untimely death left the world of reggae music a whole lot poorer.

The album concluded with the highly regarded offering of **'Johnny Gunman'** from Jackie Edwards. Other hits followed for Jackie including 'In Paradise'. Jackie was a prolific songwriter and his talents were demonstrated with the songs penned for The Spencer Davis Group in 1965, providing them with two popular number ones in the UK, 'Keep On Running' and 'Somebody Help Me Please'.

STRAIGHTEN UP FROM PAMA

Pama and Trojan began putting out compilation budget priced reggae albums in 1969, Trojan with their 'Tighten Up' series and Pama with their greatest hits from Pama's subsidiary labels, both featuring a collection of hits from the previous year. 'Tighten Up' was a massive success for Trojan with volume 2 reaching number two in the UK album chart, alas only to disappear from the chart after a couple of weeks as budget priced albums were then excluded from the chart.

The art work for Trojan featured scantily clad young ladies but Pama who had traditionally used shots of singers and club scenes on their album covers went a step further with sleeves often more explicit than Trojan. The first 'Straighten Up' from Pama was released in 1971 a good two years after the inaugural 'Tighten Up' from Trojan with the third released towards the end of 1972.

STRAIGHTEN UP VOLUME 1   PMP 2002   Released 1971

Side 1
1. LET IT BE   The Mohawks
2. LAST GOODBYE   Norman T Washington
3. WITHOUT MY LOVE   Little Roy
4. GOT TO GET YOU OFF MY MIND   Shel Alterman
5. CHARIOT COMING   The Viceroys
6. STRAIGHTEN UP   The Maytones

Side 2
1. GIVE HER ALL THE LOVE I'VE GOT   John Holt
2. BRING BACK YOUR LOVE   Owen Grey
3. YELLOW BIRD   Winston Groovy
4. SOMEDAY WE'LL BE TOGETHER   The Marvels
5. TOO EXPERIENCED   Winston Francis
6. PICK YOUR POCKET   The Versatiles

THE HISTORY OF SKINHEAD REGGAE 1968-1972   STRAIGHTEN UP

STRAIGHTEN UP VOLUME 2 PMP 2007 Released 1971

Side 1
1. GUILTY   Tiger
2. JUST MY IMAGINATION   Dave Barker
3. FAREWELL MY DARLING   Eugene Paul
4. DON'T YOU WEEP   Max Romeo
5. JOHN CROW SKANK   Derrick Morgan
6. FREE THE PEOPLE   Winston Groovy
7. MY GIRL   Slim Smith

Side 2
1. MONKEY SPANNER   Larry And Lloyd
2. LOVE AND EMOTION   The Righteous Flames
3. PUT YOUR SWEET LIPS   Raphael Stewart
4. I WANNA BE LOVED   Winston Groovy
5. CHEERIO BABY   The Classics
6. SAME THING FOR BREAKFAST   Winston & Pat
7. EVERY NIGHT   Rudy & Richards

STRAIGHTEN UP VOLUME 3 PMP 2014 Released 1972

Side 1
1. RUM RHYTHM   Shirley & Charmers
2. SOUTH OF THE BORDER   Denzil Dennis
3. NANNY SKANK   Hugh Roy
4. BEND DOWN LOW   The Groovers
5. OWEN GRAY GREATEST HITS   Owen Gray
6. ROCK STEADY   The Marvels
7. A SUGAR   Roy Shirley

Side 2
1. PRAY FOR ME   Max Romeo
2. LINGER A WHILE   John Holt
3. AILY AND AILALOO   Ninney & Max
4. SEARCHING SO LONG   Derrick Morgan
5. WAY DOWN SOUTH   Hugh Roy
6. NOTHING CAN SEPARATE US   Owen Gray
7. PLENTY OF ONE   Derrick Morgan

THE HARDER THEY COME   ISLAND RECORDS   ILPS 9202   1972

The Harder They Come soundtrack,
Original recording re-mastered available on Island Records

THE HARDER THEY COME

West Kingston Jamaica, a shanty town, on a small island in the Caribbean where the best grass in the world it was said sold for 2 dollars an ounce in the street, a place where reggae was born and where hundreds of kids flock from all over Jamaica drawn by the promise of fame and fortune.

It was here that the raw world of reggae and Jamaica was brought to the big screen for the first time. Jimmy Cliff declaring 'You Can Get It If You Really Want' portrayed one of those kids, Ivanhoe 'Ivan' Martin a non fictional young man looking for his break in music, the only way to escape from the ghetto and shanty towns.

The sound track introduced reggae to the world, a world that the skinheads had embraced since late 1968, but it also brought the harsh reality of the shanty towns of Jamaica to the fore with undeniably one if not the best ever collection of authentic reggae sounds put together on one album.

The opening track by Jimmy Cliff declares that **'You Can Get It If You Really Want'** a tracked penned by Jimmy Cliff himself. **'Draw You Brakes'** by Scotty portrays the grief that ensues in the heart of the Jamaican ghetto. The Melodians **'Rivers Of Babylon'** and **'Many Rivers To Cross'** continues the theme of oppression.

A change of tempo from Toots And The Maytals who feature in the film, comes with **'Sweet And Dandy'** a song about a young couple about to get married, having last minute nerves. The first side of the album concludes with the title track **'The Harder They Come'**.

Side two tells the story of the rude boy walking down the road with a pistol in his waist, **'Johnny Too Bad'** warn the Slickers. Crime runs through the shanty towns echoing the incessant rhythms of the sound of reggae. Desmond Dekker tells of the 'rudie' route, looting, shooting and wailing in shanty town with his hit **'007'**.

Another track to feature from Toots And The Maytals is the vivacious **'Pressure Drop'** followed by the emotively slower paced **'Sitting In Limbo'**, the track features at a very poignant moment in the film. The album concludes with an instrumental version of **'You Can Get It If You Really Want'** followed by **'The Harder They Come'** a very appropriate track portraying the end of the film and the closing credits.

Written by Perry Henzell and Trevor D. Rhone, and produced by Perry Henzell, the film is based on a true story of a character called Rhyging, a real-life Jamaican criminal who achieved fame and notoriety in the 1940's. Ivanhoe Martin is a poor Jamaican young man in search of a job, finally getting to cut a reggae record. Upon the release of his first single he discovers the only way he can get a hit record is by signing away the rights. Eventually Jose, played by Carl Bradshaw one of the first people Ivan met after he moved to Kingston offers him an opportunity to earn money drug running. He turns to a life of crime and violence.

The Harder They Come was the first feature film produced in Jamaica. The movie is in Jamaican Patois which can be understood to some extent by English speakers. There are subtitles in English for much of the original movie.

Picture the scene if you can outside the Carib Theatre in Kingston Jamaica, when the first screening of 'The Harder They Come' was due to take place. By 1pm a large crowd started gathering, despite the film scheduled for later that evening and by 6pm the crowd was estimated to have swollen to tens of thousands with traffic at a standstill. By the time it was all over the doors had been ripped from their hinges with three people to a seat, and many were torn up. The vastness of the crowds who had gathered there to witness for the first time Jamaican's on the big screen prevented many, including Jimmy Cliff, attending with even the prime minister said to have shared a single seat with his wife.

Perry Henzell had achieved success with the film, a production that had taken three years to complete with what has been described as a limited budget that kept running out, untrained actors and at times ad hoc dialogue. Despite the success in his homeland many critics advised against promoting the film overseas. Some four year ago the youth in Britain had warmed to the sounds of Jamaica but how would the people react to the film, the test would be the first screening in Brixton. The UK premier could not have been more different than that opening night in Jamaica, with many critical of the films portrayal of poverty and drug running, not their vision of sundrenched beaches and a land of milk and honey.

Attendances steadily improved and 'The Harder They Come' became a London phenomenon, in due course spreading through Europe and the World. Today 40 years on the film has achieved cult status, thanks to Henzell's dedication to his creation. As a boy he was educated in England at boarding school, before a stint working for the BBC ahead of returning to Jamaica in the 50s. Perry Henzell died in 2006 at Treasure Beach aged 70, an accomplished man who rightfully became a true legend in Jamaica.

The sleeve notes told how day and night the studios scattered about in shanty town turned out tunes, adding life to the incredible outpouring for a small island in the Caribbean. The sleeve notes continued to reveal that it was however a cry to stay alive telling that although everybody wants it maybe nobody wanted it as badly as the Jamaican's and certainly nobody has ever expressed that need better in song.

We reach the end of the story. A measure is still to be told in particular about Trojan's rival Pama. During the completion of the book many attempts have been made to contact the Palmer brothers who brought the authentic sounds of Jamaica to the UK via their charismatic PAMA label and compelling subsidiaries. Many famous names in the world of reggae have tried so I apologies for the omitted images from the golden age, but perhaps it can be resolved in the future, I have them all, just need permission to print.

Rosko gave us his top ten and I was going to finish with a little indulgence of my own but it is impossible to list as such a wide-ranging amount of quality recordings were issued during the period 68-72. The person who has described reggae as monotonous should maybe take time out and listen to the sounds of Desmond Dekker's, 'You Can Get It If You Really Want', Max Romeo's 'Wet Dream', 'Monkey Spanner' by Dave & Ansel Collins, 'Liquidator' from Harry J All-stars or 'Long Shot Kick The Bucket' from The Pioneers and of course Desmond's 'Israelites'. My list would just go on and on and on and would certainly include 'Love Of The Common People', 'Pickney Gal', '54-46 Was My Number' and 'Wonderful World Beautiful People'. There perhaps I've just done it?

CONCLUSION

The music that brought a sense of belonging to the skinheads by early 1972 had changed beyond all recognition from those early hard hitting sounds, with Trojan the main instigator of the sweetened recordings. Pama were still to some extent remaining faithful to the original sound but the quality of the output was a far cry from those early days and they never enjoyed the distribution of Trojan.

To make matters worse the quality clothing that had become as much a part of the skinheads identity as reggae was now being turned out in inferior quality from the manufacturers with the discerning skinhead losing faith the love affair would be over by the autumn of 1972. The clock was also ticking for both Trojan and Pama and unfortunately for reggae as we knew it.

Times winged chariot has moved on but those quality skinhead reggae sounds of 68 to 72 have stood the test of time and although nearly half a century has passed those original recordings still sound as fresh today as they did way back then. I hope the book has helped you reminisce back to a time when Desmond Dekker said, 'You Can Get It If You Really Want'.

Ben Sherman as Symarip said on the record
'Skinhead Jamboree' only cost 59/6